The Devil, Me, *and* Jerry Lee

The Devil, Me, *and* Jerry Lee

Linda Gail Lewis

With Les Pendleton

LONGSTREET
Atlanta, Georgia

To Elmo
and Mamie Lewis

Published by LONGSTREET PRESS, INC.,
a subsidiary of Cox Newspapers,
a subsidiary of Cox Enterprises, Inc.
2140 Newmarket Parkway
Suite 122
Marietta, Georgia 30067

Printed in the United States of America

1st printing, 1998

Library of Congress Catalog Card Number: 98-066365

ISBN: 1-56352-526-7

Book and jacket design by Jill Dible

Acknowledgments

To my family: Eddie, Annie, Oliver, Mary, Cecil, Mark Potter, Michael McCall, Jerry Lee, Frankie Jean, Marion Terrell, Clyde Braddock, Jr., Edna Braddock, Ralph Dolan, and Ann Dolan.

To my friends: Robert Garcia, Cathy Potter, Stephanie Potter, Kimberly Potter, Felicia Lemmons, Russell Medina, Sharla McNeil, Gary Burbank, Carol Purser, Johnny Dark, Cynthia Dougherty, Terri Muench, Steve Diamond, Mickey Collins, Phil Lowe, Tim Sampson, Julie Zane-Holzen, Dot Wiginton, Marjorie Perkins, Scott Faragher, Justin Ford, F. P. Wright, Maury O'Rourke, Chas White, Stuart Colman, Johnny Walker, Stephen Ackles, Donna Trull, Sam Phillips, Judd Phillips, Jerry Phillips, Knox Phillips, Steve Enoch, and Craig Benson.

Contents

1 Growing Up with God   1

2 Black River   7

3 The World Finds Jerry Lee   19

4 Sharing   33

5 The Bottom Is Up for Me   43

6 So We're a Little Bit Different   59

7 The Killer Returns   69

8 The Bottom Side of the Top   97

9 Of Love and Many Marriages   105

10 Even Evangelists Get Horny   115

11 Dick Clark Ages   123

12 It's Time to Try Normal   133

13 Kerrie KOs Killer's Kid Sister's Kareer   145

14 Click the Blue Suede Heels Together Three Times, Bobby   151

15 Let Me Interrupt Myself   159

16 Where Are We?   165

The Devil, Me, and Jerry Lee

Chapter One:
Growing Up with God

The small church was filled with "The Spirit" on that particular Sunday. Though I was barely five years old, I remember the incident as if were yesterday. The congregation, normally buzzing with small-talk prior to the Reverend's approach to the pulpit, was absolutely silent. As the adults present simultaneously turned their heads towards a door behind the pulpit normally reserved for choir members entering behind the preacher, a very small child was escorted by four Deacons to the front of the room.

Sitting with my brother, Jerry Lee, and our cousins, Mickey Gilley and Jimmy Swaggart, I was terrified by what happened. At first, I couldn't understand why the child was being so physically restrained by grown men. Seconds later, it became extremely clear. The boy, who probably weighed no more than fifty pounds, began to struggle to free himself. One of the men holding his arms flew away as if he had been pushed by some unseen force. Now, shaking violently, the child began cursing everyone with a voice that could not have come from a child or, for that matter, any normal person. I remember watching the horror film "The Exorcist" many years later and remarking how the possessed child's voice in the movie was extremely close to what I had heard in real life.

The preacher began arguing with the demons that were living in the boy's body. He rebuked the spirit and this tiny, innocent looking child spit at him and cursed everyone with the most offensive, aggressive bursts of obscenities you could possibly imagine. The congregation sat in stunned silence as this unbelievable spectacle continued.

After an hour of reciting Bible scriptures and the adult members of the congregation praying and laying their hands on the possessed boy, the demons departed from him and he became docile, quickly falling asleep in his mother's arms.

I was not surprised by such a scene, even though I was still just a child myself. The Holiness Church in Ferriday, Louisiana, was a battleground for good and evil. Though small in size and membership, with only fifty or so regularly in attendance, the fervor and zeal of those who worshipped there has never had an equal in my mind. The Lewis family, with its many branches, was always well represented. Besides my mother and daddy, Jerry Lee, me and our sister Frankie Jean, there were numerous aunts and uncles from both sides of the family.

And they were not what you would call spectators. As much as anyone in the congregation, they were filled with the Spirit, often speaking in tongues and laying their hands on the ill or possessed. Memories of events like these, coupled with the unrelenting faith of our mother, Mamie, are always in my mind.

Even so, after a life so far removed from my upbringing, what I have experienced pales by comparison to the battle that has been waged in my brother's mind and soul throughout his entire life. The Devil, me, and Jerry Lee have been slugging it out for a long time.

After church we would often stay for a wonderful meal, called "dinner on the ground," where everyone brought food from home, usually whatever a member thought was their "best" meal. Needless to say, there were tons of fried chicken, pork roast and every sort of fresh vegetable that one could imagine. In a community as rural as Ferriday, this was great fun for the kids who attended our church. We played games, sang in the children's choir and generally passed the day in the traditional southern manner of being seen and not heard.

Jerry Lee and the older boys tried to make time with the few girls their age who went to the church. He was personable and very handsome, generally the pick of the litter in our town.

Since my mother and her beloved sisters, Viola and Minnie-Belle, as well as her sisters-in-law Irene and Ada, were without a doubt some of the most devout members of the First Assembly of God, any church gathering was as much a family gathering as it was a time of worship. The point I'm making is that we were all close, raised pretty much alike and all had the fear of God put in us while we were still in diapers.

My daddy, Elmo Kidd Lewis, had married my mother, Mary Ethel Herron, when they were both very young. That turned out to be a pattern in our family. Daddy was a hardworking man who always tried his best to take care of us, but he had too much of a taste for hard liquor, and it plagued our family throughout most of our lives. He was not abusive in any way. He loved his children and took care of us as best he could. He had served a short stint in prison for bootlegging, but it never bothered me much to know it. During that time, making a living was tough, and a lot of men found themselves in the same position. Most of the time Daddy worked as a carpenter in and around Ferriday, but there wasn't a lot of building going on in the late 1930s.

Jerry Lee was not the oldest boy in the family. Elmo Jr., like so many others in our family, died an early and unnatural death. He and Aunt Maudine were walking down the road in Ferriday. It was not a busy road and very few cars traveled it. Maudine was really our cousin, not an aunt. She was just older than we were, so we called her that out of respect. Her momma was our true Aunt Stella, our mother's sister.

As they were walking, a farm truck passed them driving kind of slow, and they knew the man driving it. Thinking that they could hitch a ride if they could catch up to it, they raced to get in the back while it was still moving. Maudine was older and faster than Elmo. She made it. He didn't see the other vehicle flying down the road behind him until it was too late. Elmo was hit and killed by the drunk driver.

That was 1938 and he was just nine years old. Daddy was still in prison when it happened, and Momma had to make the funeral arrangements and deal with the heartache without him there. I know this haunted my parents all their lives. Momma refused to press the case against the driver; she said he would be punished far more than anything she could do to him. I think she was only too aware of what it was like to have a husband in prison, and perhaps she didn't want to be sending another woman's husband there.

Her faith was truly astounding, and she lived it. I swear,

she and her sisters almost seemed to have the presence of the Holy Maker with them all the time. I think that Daddy might have started seriously chasing the bottle shortly after Elmo Jr. died. The effects on the survivors of having a loved one taken away prematurely, especially in some violent manner, can be disastrous. I've seen it over and over in Jerry Lee's life. Elmo Jr. was just the first.

When I was about three, Momma sent Jerry Lee to fetch some rainwater so she could wash her hair. Our well water had a lot of iron and sulfur in it that gave your hair a green luster and a very unpleasant smell. The rainwater was caught and stored in a barrel over at her sister's house. Jerry was barely fifteen, but already driving, so he took the car, and me with him, to go get it. He filled up a glass jug with the water, and we started home.

A short ways down the road, the pitcher started to fall over in the seat. Jerry bent over to catch it and didn't see the big truck in front of us come to an unexpected stop. We slammed into the back of it. Jerry wasn't hurt, the car wasn't hurt bad, but I hit my head on the rear-view mirror and split it wide open. I was bleeding like a stuck pig when Jerry rushed me home to Momma. She saw Jerry Lee carrying me towards the house and met us at the door. She saw the blood all over my head, my dress completely saturated with it, and me lying quiet in Jerry Lee's arms. She started yelling at Jerry Lee, "You've killed my baby, you've killed my baby girl!" With Elmo Jr. having been killed, she must have lived in dread of something happening to one of the rest of us.

All the commotion scared me, and I started screaming and crying, which upset Momma even more. Jerry Lee looked me right in the face and said, "Linda Gail, shut up!" I guess it startled me so that I shut right up. They took me to the hospital and gave me about seven stitches in the head. Momma said the doctor remarked about how I didn't cry at all. He didn't know that Jerry Lee had already scared the fear out of me.

That was probably the first experience I had that showed me Jerry Lee's natural ability to take charge of people's emotions. It's got to be something in his voice or some type of charisma. I can feel it in his music. I think that ability is some of what makes his songs unique. It's a type of power.

Shortly after that Jerry Lee had another crash in the family car, this time completely ruining it. We didn't have any insurance and no money for another one. Poor old Daddy literally had to ride a bicycle to work for a long time before he could afford another car. He didn't fuss at Jerry Lee about it and never complained about having to ride the bike, even though he was a grown man. It's things like that I remember the most about Daddy. He did everything for his family. Not that he didn't have his weaknesses; the bottle was still working on him, and it would eventually cause Momma and Daddy to split up.

Chapter Two:
Black River

After about a year of hard labor, Daddy got out of prison and started working as a carpenter again. He was never lazy, and we were aware how hard he worked to keep the family going. When building slowed a bit, Daddy decided to try his hand at sharecropping. He never made any secret of the fact that he loved farming. So, with the kids in absolute depression over leaving Ferriday, we moved to the Black River community, about a half-hour drive from town. As rural as Ferriday was, it was practically downtown Manhattan compared to Black River.

To get to Black River, you have to take Hwy 20 out of Ferriday towards Alexandria, cross the Black River and take the first left, then follow this blacktop road for about fifteen miles or so till it turns into a gravel road and finally a dirt path. It ended just past our house.

Actually it wasn't a house; it was just barely a shack.

No insulation, almost no paint visible anywhere, and the only bathroom was the proverbial outhouse, a smelly hole in the ground surrounded by four rough-planked walls that served mainly to keep the wind out and the smell in. There's no smell in the world like an outhouse on a freezing cold January morning when you have to run down the path in a bathrobe just to relieve yourself. Though there may be some real character building experiences in being poor, this one never struck me as having any virtue worthy of drawing from in later life. The place just smelled liked shit.

If we had grown up in that old shack, maybe we wouldn't have known any better, so we might not have realized how badly we were living. I was mortified to get on the school bus and have everyone see where I lived. This is not to say that we didn't have some good times there. Momma and Daddy loved us and always told us we were headed for greatness. They never wavered in that belief, no matter how bad things got.

The shack was cold in the winter and hot in the summer, and the farm, without the benefit of tractors and farm hands, continuously demanded our help. We all worked in the field picking crops. All of us, that is, except Jerry Lee. He never felt a need to get his hands dirty. He had other plans in mind.

The Black River itself was a mysterious, snake-filled ribbon of darkness that wound through the cypress trees and Spanish moss for miles. We NEVER swam in it. Common sense would not allow anyone to venture into that water.

Jerry and Frankie Jean used to take an old rowboat and head up river a ways to study a very bizarre family that lived in one of the few shacks that was worse than ours. We had been told that these people had come from Africa and practiced voodoo, among other strange goings-on that seemed so outlandish at that time. Other than some odd music, the most interesting thing Jerry and Frankie Jean discovered was a peculiar habit the occupants had of going to the bathroom out the window. Looking back on it, and having already described the routine bathroom facilities that all the sharecropper shacks had, maybe it wasn't that outrageous after all. Hell, they might of done it only when they knew they were being watched by a couple of nosy neighbors. Kind of a "piss on you" gesture. Jerry Lee and Frankie Jean always got a lot of mileage out of the story though, and I remember they delighted in repeating it.

Living in Black River was hard for kids. I never made any friendships because nobody's folks wanted their children playing around or staying at somebody's house in that community. It was too far from Ferriday for my friends to come out, not that they were standing in line to visit me. I still had almost no friends and was a very lonely young girl.

Frankie Jean had a friend named Joyce. They were very close and, living like we had to, just having a good friend meant a lot. Joyce was about fifteen, the same as Frankie Jean. Frankie knew that Joyce was being physically abused at home. She was the proverbial Cinderella, providing all the family labor. Most everyone lived about like we did, and there was always something unpleasant to be done — chopping firewood, fieldwork, taking care of the animals, and even carrying out pee-pots if they had elderly folks living with them who weren't able to walk down the path to the outhouse. Joyce provided these sort of services to an ungrateful family.

She soon fell in love with a young man from Ferriday, and

they wanted to get married. Her parents, not wanting to lose the free help at the house, refused to grant their permission. Many underage girls married back then, even though they had to have their parents' permission. Distraught over the denial of her family and her depressing home-life in general, Joyce threw herself into Black River, and days passed before her bloated body was found. It was a horrible, tragic sight when they pulled her from the water. I'm sure it affected my feelings about the Black River then and even now.

There were some fun times in Black River too, not because of where we were, but because of the nature of the members of our family. Frankie Jean was, and is, just as strong-willed as Jerry Lee. She had a temper and wouldn't back down from anybody once she got her dander up. She loved Jerry Lee and I think she enjoyed getting into pissing contests with him. It was normally pretty good-natured fun, but there were several times that really stick out in my mind.

Once they got into an argument over something silly — I don't even remember what they were fussing about. But I do remember the fight that followed. Jerry Lee admired Elvis, and he had just gotten a shirt that looked like the big collared, bright colored ones that Elvis wore. He loved that shirt, and as poor as we were, it was not an easy thing to come by. They started out just fussing, then one slapped the other. Of course, there was a return slap, then a third, a fourth, and so on. It eventually turned into a wrestling match that Frankie Jean got the best of. When the fight ended, only the cuffs of that shirt remained on Jerry Lee's body. The rest had become a rag. From then on, we all said, "Don't screw with Frankie Jean unless you are in the mood for serious trouble."

When I was very young, my mother was always commenting about what pretty little hands I had. I think it finally got to the point that Frankie Jean really had heard enough about my beautiful hands, so naturally, she took me over to the oven and helped me to place them directly on the hot grates inside. I still have several nice scars on them from that skirmish.

Jerry Lee was not an angel by any means. I have heard the story numerous times from my mother about Jerry Lee almost killing one of our young cousins. He was the ringleader of a group of older boys that put this youngster in a box and left it out *on the road*! Yes, it did get hit by a car, and no, the boy wasn't seriously hurt — just bruises and a radical change in disposition. Momma was very good at straightening out Jerry Lee when he pulled something like that. He never did anything intentional to hurt anybody after that.

Not too much later, I put my family through a night of hell. Late one night, long after Jerry Lee, Frankie Jean and I had gone to bed, my mother happened by our bedroom door. Like any concerned mother, she couldn't resist looking in on us to make sure we were all right. She noticed I wasn't in the bed. She checked out the whole house, as tiny as it was, only to find that I was nowhere to be found. Then she went outside, in just her robe on a freezing night, and ran down to the outhouse to make sure I didn't have some sort of bowel attack after I went to bed. Nope, nothing there but the cold smell of decaying shit. She was really getting scared by then.

Now, our community offered nothing in the way of entertainment to tempt a young girl out at that time of night. So Momma began to reason that the Rapture had come and Jesus had taken me to heaven. She just couldn't understand why he took only me and left everybody else. After all, the church was practically her entire life. By using that logic, she reconsidered her Rapture theory and started to get scared again. She began to think that I had been kidnapped or raped and thrown in the river. She got everybody up to look for me.

After a frantic half-hour, all the noise must have woke me up from my resting place in the *clothes hamper*! Apparently I had been sleepwalking, something I never did before or since, and I finally fell asleep in the clothes hamper. I'll never figure that one out. Daddy said all he could think of was that young girl's body floating down the river. Even Jerry Lee was a nervous wreck. I guess it's times like that when you find out who really loves you.

#

There was this old piano that Daddy's sister, Eva, and her husband, Uncle Harvey, had bought for their daughter, Norma Jean. When Jerry saw it the first time, Momma said he just walked up to it and started playing. No lessons, no reason for him to be able to do it. But there it was. As fate surely dictated, Norma Jean didn't take much interest in the piano, and her folks made it possible for Daddy to buy it for us. I know we didn't have any money then, and I always heard that they let us have it on some sort of credit. Whatever the arrangement was, it was definitely the turning point in all of our lives.

I'll never forget, my daddy carried it down from their second-floor apartment and into our house all by himself, and it had to weigh a ton. It was one of those old uprights that looked like it should be in the saloon of "Gunsmoke" or on a riverboat in "Maverick." Daddy was as proud as I ever saw him, to get that for his kids.

And nobody ever had a gift for the piano like Jerry Lee. He was a child prodigy. This wasn't something that he just familiarized himself with when he became a teenager so that he could become a musician. That wasn't the case at all. That first piano has a special place in all of our lives. My sister Frankie Jean still has it in the Lewis Family Museum in Ferriday.

From the very start, Jerry Lee threw himself into music, and he had the gift. As hard as it is to believe, considering our circumstances, Momma and Daddy literally groomed their children for stardom. If they had known how unlikely it was that any of us would ever make it as a big-time entertainer, they might have given up. The fact that they were so naïve was probably a big factor in Jerry Lee's becoming a success. Like a kid in West Virginia whose parents hope that he'll get a football scholarship and escape the coal mines, our parents saw in Jerry's music a future, a way out of the desperate poverty that we were living in.

I'll tell you something that I doubt a lot of you will believe, but it's the truth: My mother picked cotton the day she gave birth to me and gave the money to Jerry Lee to go to a club. His entire life had been a fairly unusual affair. Pretty much everybody in the area around Ferriday knew that Jerry Lee was . . . well, different from most people.

Even as a young teenager, he could enter a room full of people and everybody would just stop in their tracks and look at him. He had this presence. He wasn't then, or now, the silly, lighthearted character portrayed in the movie, "Great Balls of Fire." If anything, he was always the heavy. He's sort of a brooder — moody, temperamental and completely spoiled. He's had his ass kissed by just about everybody his whole life. That has to have an impact on anybody.

Still, he loved his family, and deep inside he's always been a caring person.

By his early teens, he could stop a train with his piano playing. He had been entered in talent contests all around the state and won them all. Even though gospel music had been a constant around our house and Jerry could do it great, he always liked to play things a little more up-tempo than most people were expecting. To borrow an old saying, he was "*Born to boogie*." He could play just about every style of music, from gospel and country to classical. Momma and Daddy never said "if" Jerry Lee makes it, they always just said "when" he makes it.

Cousin Jimmy Swaggart wasn't far behind Jerry on the piano. When they were just barely in their teens, the church rented two pianos and put them back to back in the church for one of the most unbelievable duets ever. As good as they were, nobody there, other than Momma and Daddy, ever dreamed what lay ahead for the Lewis family.

Jerry went to school only through the ninth grade. The girls all loved him and he was very popular. Once he decided to give sports a try. After all, girls loved sports stars, too. He became the running back on the football team after just a short while. Apparently he was as fast on his feet as he was on the keyboard. He was doing great until he broke his leg, and that ended his stint as an athlete once and for all. He wore his leg cast like a badge of honor and milked it for all it was worth with the girls.

It was apparent from very early on that Jerry Lee needed a woman — at least one, and more was even better. The times and the place we were living in demanded that you be married before you started hitting the sack with somebody. It seems, at this early age, that Jerry Lee must have been influenced by that tradition and was determined to follow it. By sixteen, Jerry Lee had taken his first bride, Dorothy. She was the preacher's daughter and very attractive. She was a sweet girl and just worshipped Jerry Lee. He swears to this day that she was the only virgin he has ever been with in his life.

Unfortunately, Jerry's wandering eye and desire for the wild side of life brought that marriage to a quick demise. He would never be able to be faithful to one woman, not then or ever. Dorothy truly loved Jerry Lee. She married one time after their divorce, and it didn't last very long either. There's no doubt in my mind that she always loved Jerry Lee.

Jerry went through several quick marriages during the next couple of years. He was tempted continually, and he just didn't like to say no. The second one was Jane, who could best be described as a "fast woman." She was sexy, loose, and as wild as Jerry Lee. He probably deserved this one. It was a stormy and short-lived affair also. She was running around practically from day one.

One of Jerry Lee's oldest and lifelong friends is Cecil Harrelson. They met in grade school and have remained close till today. Cecil is as much family as anybody could be. Cecil was about twelve when I was born. Nobody could have ever guessed, especially me, that he and I would eventually get married . . . twice.

Cecil and Jerry both loved music and had a similar thirst for the wild side. They began going to clubs together, and before too long they determined that the music business was in their future. Cecil was never a musician, but he later became Jerry's road manager. He went with him to a lot of the small clubs early on, as much to be with Jerry as for any other reason. Jerry trusted him with anything. Since they had no car or money, they spent most of the time on foot.

They even slept in ditches for lack of a better option.

It was about this time that Jerry Lee began working the clubs around the Natchez, Mississippi, area. Two of the better known joints were the "Blue Cat Club" and the "Wagon Wheel." These were not only juke joints of the first order, but you could drink at any age if you could order and pay. You could pick up a woman, get laid and killed or all three in the same evening.

Momma and Daddy knew what was going on, and Momma didn't like it at all. Her strict religious beliefs went dead against such places. However, that's where the music was being played that Jerry Lee was attracted to. There were very few things, almost none, in fact, that Jerry Lee was willing to do against his mother's wishes. This was one.

Back then, the hottest thing going was the boogie woogie. Jerry Lee and Cecil had met a blind piano player named Mr. Paul, and Jerry actually began playing the drums for him. This became Jerry Lee's first band. Jerry wasn't even the lead singer in the beginning. That position was handled by Johnny Little John, whose greatest claim to fame could be that he taught Jerry Lee "Whole Lotta Shakin' Goin' On." It didn't take long, however, for them to find out where the talent was. Jerry would do a number on the piano, and nobody ever considered trying to follow him on the keyboard. It was apparent to everyone who heard him, even then, that he had great talent.

Jerry became a big draw in the Natchez area. There wasn't a lot of money in it, but he was married and he had to make what he could. As far as I can remember, Jerry Lee has never made a dime in his life from anything other than music. Wait a minute – there was that time he tried to sell Singer sewing machines. They were getting real popular in the South and everybody wanted one. Very few families could afford to just go to a clothing store and pick out what they wanted, so new dresses usually came in the form of patterns and raw material from the department store.

Jerry Lee decided that he could make a little extra money selling sewing machines door-to-door around Ferriday. So he got a brochure from the company that had some nice pictures in it and started doing just that. His charisma as an entertainer carried over into the sewing machine business real well, and he sold quite a few of these fine machines. The only problem was, he didn't have any to sell! He spent the money as quick as he took it in and never ordered the first one. Now, I believe that he truly intended to make good on these sales, but he just got caught in a tight spot. After a couple of weeks, folks started wanting to know when their sewing machines would be arriving. He knew he should quit and try and make it right to these "neighbors" who trusted him, but the money was too good.

Before too long, some of the customers undoubtedly got suspicious and alerted the local sheriff. Now, the sheriff knew us, as did everybody in town, and he came to ask Jerry Lee the appropriate questions. Jerry Lee didn't have the appropriate answers, so Momma and Daddy were brought into it. The only way that Jerry Lee wasn't going to jail was to produce a whole bunch of sewing machines awfully fast or to refund everybody's money. Momma and Daddy flat out didn't have the money. Jerry Lee was sweating bullets and could already see himself in stripes. That's when good old Uncle Lee, our favorite relative in the whole world, came through as he had done so many times before.

He never had a family of his own, and he just loved us to

death. He had married Aunt Stella, Momma's sister, and sort of adopted all of us. I know that many years we would not have had any Christmas at all if it weren't for him. He's dead and gone now, but I just hope he knew how much he meant to us.

The folks who bought the sewing machines all got their money back, and Jerry Lee never tried to make a dollar doing anything but music for the rest of his life. That has probably been good for everyone.

Chapter Three:
The World Finds Jerry Lee

Jerry Lee was playing the piano and singing every night at one joint or another. He was hooked for life. To this day, these small clubs hold the best memories for Jerry Lee. That's a pretty big statement for someone who has headlined at Vegas, on prime time TV and just about every concert hall in the world. For years, after long tours of concert halls and arenas, Jerry Lee would come home and play for free in these honky-tonks. Some of those impromptu jam sessions have become legendary around Memphis.

Though Momma and Daddy didn't endorse where Jerry Lee was playing, they still encouraged his efforts as a musician. Around 1955, Cecil paid for Jerry Lee to make an acetate recording, the first Jerry Lee ever made. It cost two dollars and he sang "Don't Stay Away Too Long Darlin', 'Cause Love Grows Cold". On the other side, he played a solo piano rag. Only Cecil, Jerry Lee and a fanatic Jerry Lee fan from England have ever heard it. Cecil has it to this very day. God only knows what it's worth.

Mickey Gilley and Jimmy Swaggart weren't distant cousins. They were around a lot and hung out with Jerry Lee and Cecil. Their mothers were all close and were the ringleaders at the church. I guess it would come as no surprise to anyone to hear that Jimmy's mother was almost fanatical in her beliefs. Nonetheless, she was a sweet and a quiet woman who loved her family.

Jimmy's daddy, Uncle Son, was a different story. He was fanatical too, but he was also abusive to the kids. He beat them at the drop of a hat and generally scared the shit out of them and the religion into them. I can remember going to the movie in Ferriday on a Friday night when everyone, including Jimmy, would wait in line to buy their tickets. When everyone else went in, Jimmy would have to leave. Uncle Son wouldn't let him go in. He considered the movies evil. Hell, our preacher had said that television antennas were the Devil's tail.

It's a miracle we're all not more fucked up than we are. I know it had to be embarrassing for Jimmy. He wasn't a big-time evangelist then — just a kid — and it had to hurt. I feel to this day that the troubles he got into with prostitutes later in his life can be traced back to his upbringing. The worse thing that came out of that whole embarrassing episode is having so many people think that Jimmy is just another money-grubbing fraud. That's not it at all. Jimmy is as sincere as a person can be. He believes what he preaches deeply, and it really makes me feel bad for him.

He always had Jerry Lee's soul on his mind, and it has worried him sick to see all that Jerry Lee has gone through. On numerous occasions, when Jerry Lee struck rock bottom and was just about dead from abusing drugs, Jimmy would come to get him and put him in a rehab clinic to dry out. He would beg him to come back to the church, and for a while he would. It just never stuck.

Uncle Son put Jimmy through plenty of hell himself. Kids carry that kind of indoctrination with them forever. Uncle Son was actually the son of Daddy's sister, Ada, which made Jimmy a double cousin. Later on, when people asked me if I thought it was a little bit weird that Jerry Lee married his first cousin, I'd always say, "Hell, in Ferriday, I could have married a cousin and not even known it. It was no big deal."

Jimmy is actually our double cousin; his mother, Minnie Bell, is my mother's sister, and his father is my Daddy's nephew. Got it?

Mickey Gilley was the son of Daddy's sister Irene and Uncle Arthur Gilley. Two of Daddy's sisters married brothers. Irene married Arthur, and Aunt Eva married his brother Harvey. This would probably be a bit confusing to some folks, but it always seemed pretty normal to me. Our family tree was actually more of a vine than a tree.

Uncle Arthur drove a cab and they didn't have much money either, but Mickey always had his eyes on a buck. He's damn good at it, too. If he had managed Jerry Lee's money for him, there's no telling how rich he could have been. I know that Mickey is more wealthy than anyone who was raised in Ferriday could possibly imagine. Money was always more important to Mickey and Jimmy than it was to Jerry Lee. Whenever Jerry Lee had it, he just gave it away to his family and the people around him.

Jimmy Swaggart's wife, Frances, is a good woman — a little rigid but very decent. I remember once they were visiting with us at Aunt Irene's (Mickey's momma's rooming house) and he turned to her and asked her where her pocketbook was. She said she left it in the car, and I swear, he knocked the shit out of her. He literally knocked her to the ground. If there's one thing you don't do, it's mess around with Jimmy's money. Still, he's a product of the same environment as Jerry Lee, and I admire the way he's put it all together and kept his perspective on things. He's still got a lot of the traits that Jerry Lee has, though. One in particular is women.

If there's one thing that all the Lewises — Mickey and Jimmy and Jerry Lee and even I — have in common, it's sex. We're definitely over-sexed. Not that it's a bad thing. I think between Jerry Lee and myself, we've had fifteen fairly interesting marriages. I've had eight husbands and Jerry Lee has had seven brides. Now, a lot of people have asked me, "Why in the world would you marry eight times?" I always reply, "Well, you can't marry everybody you have sex with. Let's be realistic!"

Still, that's a hell of a lot of courting, and there were certainly a lot of times when getting married just wasn't a consideration. I always felt a little like Liz Taylor, who said she thought she should marry anybody she was sleeping with. Looking back on it, I think about four less marriages and a little more sleeping would have been a good number. And, God forgive me for marrying the Elvis impersonator. I would like to take the time to apologize right now for that little episode. We'll look a little closer at that tragedy later on.

By 1954, Jerry Lee was exploding with talent. He had all

those great gifts and a way with women that was pretty much unequaled. He just needed a record deal. Elvis was getting started, and Jerry Lee could just see himself every time he heard Elvis. He knew he could rock 'n' roll better than anybody. He convinced Daddy, not that it was all that hard, that he just had to go to Nashville and show the record companies what he could do.

Like most everybody in the South, we were raised listening to WSM and the Grande Ole Opry, not to forget our own Louisiana Hayride. The influence was all country. Hell, you didn't get much more country than we were. Jerry also had a large musical influence courtesy of Haney's Big House right there in Ferriday. It was a black club where the best black musicians of the time played every night. Mr. Haney liked Jerry Lee and would let him slip in and listen. Just like Elvis, Jerry Lee had a lot of soul influence in his music. You can hear it and feel it in both their voices.

So, the next order of business was to get enough money together to help Jerry Lee make the trip to Tennessee. A lot of credence has been given to the popular version of the story that has Jerry Lee gathering eggs to finance the trip. I'm not saying that eggs weren't gathered — a hell of a lot of eggs were gathered — I'm just saying that Jerry Lee was not the *gatheree*. As Butterfly McQueen said in *Gone With the Wind*, "It were mostly me." There, I finally got it off my chest. When the money was finally "laid," Daddy and Jerry Lee got in the old wreck and made the trip north. That was early in 1956.

Jerry Lee was thrilled to get to Nashville, but his youthful confidence was apparently not appreciated by the handful of record company executives who owned country music at that time. Nashville has always been clannish and a good-ole-boy town. Country music was rigidly controlled by just a few men. It didn't matter how great you were — if they didn't get interested in your career, it just wouldn't happen. They were what you could call "Big Shits." To put it mildly, Jerry Lee was never awestruck by anybody. If they wanted talent, he had it, but humble pie was not there.

The one piece of "constructive" advice they offered him was forget the piano and learn to play the guitar. And so, he got the quick boot from the entire town. RCA, Decca, Capitol all passed. He was too flamboyant, too up tempo, too everything, and Nashville never was a progressive town when it came to music. Jerry was not the first great talent they had passed on, and certainly he won't be the last.

Somewhat discouraged, Jerry Lee begged Daddy to go through Memphis on the way home. He had heard that a man named Sam Phillips had signed Elvis, and Jerry Lee loved Elvis. No matter what was ever said about competition between them or any hard feelings, Jerry Lee Lewis always loved Elvis and his music. They would become friends for life. Phillips had to have an open mind to have signed someone as different as Elvis, so they decided to give it a try.

Sam Phillips was the founder, owner and genius behind Sun Records. He was in the midst of turning the music world on its ear. Probably because of the influence of black music in the Memphis clubs and the different sort of music that was coming from there, Phillips had a much broader ear for music than most of the other producers of that time. He basically believed that a white man with a black soul would be a huge success. Whatever his reasoning, it worked. In quick succession, he would "discover" Elvis, Roy Orbison, Johnny Cash, Carl Perkins and Jerry Lee Lewis. No matter what is ever said about Sam, he had a vision for the future of music.

As luck would have it, Sam was in Florida when Daddy and Jerry arrived and wouldn't be back for a couple of weeks. His friend and associate Jack Clements was managing the store, so to speak. Unlike the great minds in Nashville, he was cordial and agreed to audition Jerry Lee. After a quick listen to Jerry Lee's unheard-of arrangement of "Crazy Arms," Jack decided to tape him and play it for Sam when he came home. He promised that they'd hear from them. Jerry Lee was high with enthusiasm, because he knew he had impressed Jack Clements.

As quick as that, Jerry Lee and Daddy were back home. Nobody ever said it, but I think they felt like Jerry Lee might not get the chance he needed. Having so many supposedly knowledgeable entertainment gurus tell them to forget it had depressed them. It apparently was not enough to be merely great; you also had to be just what they saw as a marketable artist, and their vision was *extremely* limited.

Several anxious weeks went by. Then, late one afternoon, Aunt Stella came by the house to tell us, "They've called Jerry Lee from Memphis."

Jerry Lee flipped out. "I knew it! I knew they'd be calling."

In looking back on it, I can't decide whether providence intervened or whether great talent will eventually find a way. Whatever was at work here, things were looking up.

Almost immediately, Jerry Lee was back in Memphis recording "Crazy Arms" for Sam Phillips. From the very first, Sam Phillips loved Jerry Lee Lewis. He has said many times to a lot of different folks that Jerry Lee was the greatest talent he ever heard. Considering the talent that he discovered, that was saying a hell of a lot.

"Crazy Arms" got very little airplay. One of the few

industry stars who heard anything special in it was Conway Twitty. He said that he recognized immediately that Jerry Lee was a unique musician. Jerry assembled a small band to start playing the gigs that were available after the modest response to his first record. The group consisted of J.W. Brown on bass and Russell Smith on drums. For about six months, they traveled from town to town doing one-nighters for small clubs.

I was in the third grade at the time. My teacher asked the students to tell about something that had happened to them that they thought the rest of the class would be interested in hearing. I told them that my brother had just made a record. To me, it was quite remarkable, but they just stared at me like I was from another planet. I was beginning to feel different from the rest of the kids I knew. I never fit in there, and so I dreamed about places a long way off.

My family was so excited for Jerry Lee. We didn't have much going for us and still not enough money to live even close to decent. Even so, there was some resentment from the community, and some just thought we were plain old crazy. To even suggest that Jerry Lee Lewis was going to be a big star was ridiculous and farfetched. Most of the people in town knew Jerry Lee and realized that he was extremely talented, but that sort of ambition just didn't seem to fit in Ferriday. I was growing quickly tired of the learning environment.

By eleven, I had the body of a grown woman. I was playing around with beer, cigarettes, driving a car and entertaining a number of boys. The Lewis hormones were raging. Money was still tight at home.

Jerry Lee and his second wife Jane were still living in Ferriday. In all truthfulness, I have to say that Jane was sporting around town with a number of young studs while Jerry Lee was on the road. She was beautiful and wild. She loved the men and they loved her back. She became pregnant with Ronnie. There was no way of proving who Ronnie's father was back then — DNA testing was unheard of — but Jerry Lee knew she had been running around and strongly suspected that the child was not his.

I know he felt concerned that Jane had a small child, but it was not going to slow him down. Ronnie was sent to live with Jane's sister, Jewel, and Jerry Lee moved to Memphis to be closer to his career and the Sun studio. Jane remained in Ferriday.

Jerry Lee started staying with J.W. Brown, who played in the band with him. J.W. was married to Daddy's sister. This put Jerry Lee in daily contact with his sexy little cousin Myra. He stayed with them for several months until Jane demanded that he get a place so she could move up there with him.

Even though Jane moved to Memphis and they got a small house together, the marriage quickly fell apart. Our cousin Myra was waiting in the wings to take Jerry Lee on the ride of his young life.

A lot has been said and written about Jerry Lee being twenty years old and him taking advantage of his young, thirteen-year-old cousin. First off, Myra looked like she was twenty, and she was definitely not a virgin. Jerry Lee was not the first man she had been with. She was more than a bit on the wild side herself. I know this for a fact, because she showed that side to my sister Frankie Jean, who didn't appreciate it at all. They were the same age and hung out together while Jerry Lee was on the road. And just where were J.W. and his wife when Jerry Lee and

Myra were "getting it on" just a few feet away in their tiny little house? You'll never convince me they didn't know what was going on. As Sam Phillips said, "It's just about money."

J.W. could see what was happening with Jerry Lee and knew they would benefit a great deal if he took an interest in Myra. I know that's a horrible thing to say, but I believe it's true. J.W. didn't even get upset with Jerry Lee about marrying his "baby." Jerry Lee and J.W. remain close friends to this day.

Our mother was a different story, however. She let Jerry Lee know exactly what she thought about the marriage — it was wrong and she would never approve of it. Once again, Jerry didn't listen to his mother.

#

Sam Phillips had a brother named Judd. They fought quite a bit but still communicated. Judd was in Florence, Alabama, where Jerry Lee was scheduled to play, so Sam called him up and told him that Jerry Lee Lewis was worth going to hear. Judd agreed to give them a listen.

The first meeting between Judd Phillips and Jerry Lee was rather odd, to say the least. Judd didn't let Jerry Lee know he was coming to watch him; he wanted to see Jerry when he wasn't aware somebody was there to "size" him up. Judd slipped quietly into the back of the club and listened to the show. He caught only the last few songs that evening but was blown away by what he heard. He decided to wait around and introduce himself to the band.

Jerry Lee had gone to the club owner to get the small fee they had coming. The club owner had not had a big night, however, and apparently decided that he didn't have to pay the band. That was not a good decision. As Judd approached them, Jerry Lee and J.W. began breaking chairs apart. They advised the club owner that if they didn't get their money pretty damned quick, there'd be no one sitting down in the joint unless they brought their own chair.

Judd approached them laughing out loud at the scene. Jerry Lee turned to him and said, "Just who the hell are you?" Judd told him he was Sam's brother, and Jerry said he'd have to wait a few minutes till they had finished breaking all the chairs. The club owner had seen enough and reluctantly produced a handful of cash, and the boys calmed down. Judd liked Jerry right off. They had a few drinks together and hit it off as friends.

Shortly after the meeting, Judd called Sam and told him that he believed Jerry Lee Lewis could be a big star. Judd traveled to Memphis and pressured Sam for money to promote him. Though Sam knew Jerry Lee was talented, he was having second thoughts as to whether or not the public would like him. He'd had a record out for quite some time, and it had not done very well. But after a lot of persuading, Sam finally gave Judd the go-ahead. He contacted Jerry Lee and told him to get back to Memphis. Jerry Lee came straight back. He and Judd were going to New York City so that Judd could try and get him some television exposure.

Jerry Lee was just a young kid. He packed chewing gum and comic books for the trip. The rest of the band stayed behind. There was just enough money for Judd and Jerry Lee to make the trip. After a number of rejections, Judd finally got a contact on "The Steve Allen Show" to listen to Jerry Lee. Five minutes, that was it. "The Steve Allen Show" was one of the hottest programs on the air, and every entertainer in the world would have jumped at the chance to be on it. Jerry played his new recording, a really rocking version of "Whole Lotta Shakin' Goin' On." The man was duly impressed and retrieved Steve Allen personally to hear him. Allen loved what he heard and said he wanted Jerry Lee on the following Sunday's show.

Jerry called home and we all went nuts. They agreed to pay for J.W. and Russell to go to New York and back up Jerry Lee since they were familiar with his music. Steve gave Jerry Lee the break that made him. "Whole Lotta Shakin'" had been out for six months and hadn't done shit. Jerry Lee cut loose on the show with the kind of energy and excitement that bordered on wild. Most of the people who saw the show said they would never forget that performance. His wavy blonde hair, his hands flying over the keyboard, and then he stood up, kicked the piano bench away and played like he was trying to set the keys on fire with his hands. Parents were flabbergasted — they were still hoping Elvis would disappear — and now this! But the kids everywhere flipped over his performance. Jerry Lee not only never forgot what Steve Allen did for him, he even named his next child Steve Allen Lewis.

Judd Phillips, a savvy promoter who recognized that destiny was giving him a great opportunity, called Sam Phillips and told him that he needed more cash to pay off the big-shot disc jockeys to get Jerry Lee's records played. Sam provided it, and within weeks "Whole Lotta Shakin' Goin' On" was a colossal hit record.

There are a lot of people who will tell you that this combination of breaks — getting a record deal with Sam and Sun Records, meeting Judd and then getting a shot on "The Steve Allen Show" — was a miraculous affair that Jerry Lee

Lewis was just fortunate enough to be the recipient of. All I can say to that is you don't know Jerry Lee. I believe to this day that he has a unique God-given talent that is one in millions. Everyone who ever listened to him play in person, even as a small child, knew that he had heard something extremely special. Jerry Lee would have happened no matter what. He would not have been denied.

There were doors shut in his face early on in Nashville and even more after events in his private life put him in disfavor with a lot of the public. It never stopped him, not then, not now. He didn't play for fame and fortune; he played because he loved the music and he loved to entertain, whether it was for $25,000 a night or $200. You could never tell any difference in what he put into a performance by the size of the crowd or the money he was being paid. Jerry Lee loves to play music.

Chapter Four:
Sharing

Jerry Lee had always told Momma and Daddy that when he made money, whatever he had he wanted his family to have. Shortly after he hit the top of the record charts, Sam Phillips gave him a check for $40,000. That was a special check for a lot of reasons. It was not only more money than our parents had earned in an entire lifetime of backbreaking labor, it also freed our family from the bitter well of poverty. Unfortunately, it also would be the last check that Jerry Lee ever received from Sam Phillips, even though his records would make many millions of dollars for Sam and Sun Records.

When Sam gave the check to Jerry Lee, he offered him a suggestion on how to invest the money so that he would be secure if his career didn't last very long. He told him that he should take the entire $40,000 and invest it in a new company that was being formed in Memphis. He said he knew the people involved in it and that it would certainly be a good investment. After carefully considering the advice of the man who had made Jerry Lee Lewis a household name, Jerry did exactly what he thought best. He immediately bought two new Cadillacs, a pile of new clothes and band equipment, and partied hard. I guess he figured that nothing would ever come from a company with a name as hokey as Holiday Inns of America.

Jerry Lee called home and told Momma and Daddy that he wanted them to leave everything they had in the shack at Black River and go buy a new house in Ferriday. He said Momma was to pick out whatever she wanted and to buy all new furniture. Not a single piece of the second- and third-hand junk we had in Black River did he want to see when he came home. He also sent us a thousand dollars each to go buy new clothes. There wasn't a thousand dollars worth of clothes that I could wear in all of Ferriday. That was a huge amount of money back then to spend on clothes. Momma picked out a small white framed house in town that she thought would be nice, and they bought it. In quick order, the new furniture got delivered and we moved in. We were in heaven. Jerry came home the next weekend, and when he saw the house he was not pleased with it. He was not having his folks in a dinky little frame house. He took Momma and Daddy to Ridgecrest, the newest and nicest neighborhood in town and, with her consent, picked out a beautiful brick ranch house. She loved it. It had this huge picture window that impressed me to no end. He bought it on the spot before they even sold the other one. That done, we moved into this place that was truly a palace compared to what we had been used to.

A lot of people would consider Jerry Lee's rise from obscurity to stardom nothing short of meteoric. Jerry considered it about damn time. Not that he didn't enjoy the recognition. No matter what any performer says about wanting their privacy and that the public should butt out of their lives, it's all bullshit. They want to be noticed, to be recognized and acclaimed for their talent. I always thought it ridiculous that someone would drive up in a black stretch limo with the windows tinted too dark to see through because they didn't want to draw attention to themselves. What a crock! If they didn't want attention, I say do what Howard Hughes did — get a ten-year-old Chevy with faded paint and rusted bumpers and dress like a normal human being. I guarantee that would cut their "being bothered" by ninety-nine percent. And, it ain't gonna happen. Jerry Lee was finally where he always knew he was headed. National television, ten thousand bucks a night in concert, and he was in demand everywhere, not just in the United States.

Women have thrown themselves at Jerry Lee all his life. Needless to say, when you're at the top of the charts and money is overflowing from your wallet with every step, it only gets worse. I've seen many women hand hundred dollar bills to people backstage to let them wait in Jerry Lee's dressing room so that they could offer him literally anything that came to his mind in the way of sex. What most men consider a fantasy was a daily routine for Jerry Lee. I suppose some men might be strong or gay enough not to be bothered by it, but Jerry Lee just considered it a fringe benefit of stardom.

As I mentioned earlier, Jane and Jerry Lee had been living in the house in Memphis, Jerry Lee was already having an affair with cousin Myra, and Jane was pregnant with Ronnie. Jerry Lee realized that Jane was running around on him. Jane's sister, Jewel, was raising baby Ronnie, but Jerry

Lee never accepted Ronnie as his son. I got to know Ronnie and he's a very sweet person. If there was even a chance that Ronnie was his, it was Jerry Lee's loss. It was just a matter of months before Jerry Lee and Jane separated and divorced. Jerry immediately married Myra.

It's always been interesting to me that the marriage to his thirteen-year-old cousin didn't jar the press in the United States. It was on Jerry Lee's first visit to England that the British press corps blew it up into a national scandal. It's funny how such a repressed, tight-assed, kinky country became so obsessed with the fact that Jerry Lee was screwing his cousin. Obviously, they had never studied the sleeping habits of their own royalty. Hell, half of the Kings and Queens of Europe where married to their first cousins. Nobody is just born looking like Prince Charles. It takes a lot of big noses in the family to get one like his. And today — if Jerry were just hitting the charts for the first time — he'd have to be sleeping with a basset hound to generate that kind of press. And wouldn't we all feel a lot better about Michael Jackson if he would mess around with someone as old as Myra was . . . and of the opposite sex? Everything is relative to the time you live in.

I was only ten years old when "Whole Lotta Shakin' Goin' On" became a number one record. Jerry Lee was on the road a lot, and Frankie Jean, Momma and Daddy all went on tour with him for short periods. Even though she came from a dirt-poor, small-world background, Momma made the adjustment to worldly as gracefully as anyone could have. The wannabe's in Ferriday, people who were just a little better off than we had been, were apparently resentful of our sudden prosperity. They were cruel to me at school and pretty nasty to the rest of my family. The few people in town who were rich were the nicest. They were kind to us and never acted like we were any different from anyone else.

There was one woman who was extremely kind to my mother. She was a world renowned horticulturist. She was extremely rich and lived in a beautiful home. She had Momma over to her house and was so kind to her for years. There were several other families who I remember as being particularly nice to us.

For the most part, I was going through hell at school. I had no friends at all. Looking back, it's understandable. I was very mature physically and was quickly becoming a lot more worldly than the rest of the kids. I had gotten a taste of the outside world, and I knew I would never be satisfied spending my life in Ferriday. I had the burn to be on the road like Jerry Lee. The most magical moment in my entire life had to be that first visit to Memphis, to see Jerry Lee and Myra. Jane had moved back to Ferriday and reclaimed baby Ronnie. Jerry Lee and Myra had a nice house, and I was welcome there most anytime.

Visiting Memphis was like taking someone today from Bangladesh, putting them on a 747 and whisking them up to New York City. Lights, cars, beautiful stores and nightclubs everywhere. Jerry Lee was almost always on the road, and Myra didn't go very often. I'm sure Jerry Lee preferred it that way. He never slowed down on his appetite for a wide array of bed partners. He was in his heyday, and the money flowed over Memphis like a raging green waterfall. We all felt the rewards of his talent. He continued to share with his family. Momma would remain in new Cadillacs and housekeepers till she died, no matter how well Jerry Lee was doing.

There were a number of events I remember about the early years when Jerry was a headliner. One occurred backstage at a rock 'n' roll concert promoted by the famous disc jockey, Allan Freed. There were a number of other major stars on the show, such as Chuck Berry, Fats Domino and Little Richard. Anyone who knows much about rock 'n' roll knows that Chuck Berry did as much to establish it as anyone. Daddy was with Jerry Lee on this particular trip.

Now, Jerry Lee had grown up color blind, and Momma, bless her soul, had two lovely black women who took care of her from the time Jerry first hit it big until she died. They were family to her, and she never acknowledged race in any fashion. I wish I could say the same of Daddy, but he was a product of his environment and time. Apparently, he took exception to something that Chuck Berry said and quickly produced a knife backstage as he was determined to slice him up. Allan Freed intervened immediately, saying, "I'm sorry, Mr. Lewis, but Mr. Berry is one of the stars of this show, and I just can't allow you to murder him."

Daddy replied, "Well, where I'm from, we just take care of these kind and chuck in the 'blue hole.'" The blue hole was a bottomless pit of dark blue water back in Ferriday where people tossed pretty much anything they never wanted to see again.

Mr. Freed apparently thought Daddy was just picking at Chuck Berry and didn't really mean it. That could have been a horrible mistake under a lot of circumstances. Jerry Lee got that wild streak from Daddy, and I guess he was capable of doing a lot of things that other people might not look at too favorably. Well, no harm done. Daddy and Chuck Berry were separated.

Jerry Lee followed "Whole Lotta Shakin' Goin' On" with several other rock hits, including "Great Balls of Fire," "High School Confidential," and "Breathless." At all of his concerts, though primarily attended by rock 'n' roll fans, Jerry Lee includes some purely country songs. He's always been country and never tried to hide it. While it may have turned off a few hard rockers, it would be his lifesaver in the long run.

Jerry Lee shared the stage with all the big stars of the period, and though he didn't always have the hottest record at the moment, anyone who thought they could follow him on stage and close the show quickly realized that was pretty much an impossibility. He would rev up the crowd with his driving rhythms and heart-stopping piano playing till the audience had no energy left. Anybody behind him was pretty much just providing a moment for the crowd to catch its breath. On one such night, Brenda Lee had a monster hit and demanded that she would close the show, the premier spot. Jerry Lee offered no resistance at all. "Hell, if Brenda wants to close the show, why just let her go ahead." By the time Jerry Lee wiped out the audience and Brenda Lee finished singing her number one record to a modest hand clapping, she was literally in tears. She never made the demand to close again. The word got around and most other artists never wanted to follow him either.

Another "closing" tale that comes to mind involved a show in Britain during one of Jerry Lee's heavy drug periods, about 1974. The British had long since gotten over their problems with Jerry's earlier marriage to Myra, and he was beloved throughout the UK. Although Peter Frampton was a big star at that moment, the fans in the audience were decidedly Jerry Lee fans. They were applauding, stomping their feet and still yelling "Jerry . . . Jerry" in unison as he left the stage. The chanting didn't stop for five minutes after he left. It would not have been proper etiquette for him to extend his performance, as Jerry Lee was not the official headliner; Frampton was the main act. Frampton waited for several more minutes to no avail, and finally he ran out on stage, expecting to do his gig. The audience not only booed as he took the stage, they began to throw bottles at him! Peter finally gave up and left without doing a single number. The audience literally destroyed the stage. I was not there, but Ian Wallace, a well-known music critic from London, and who is a close friend today, relayed that story to me. He spent that night sleeping on the street as he stayed so long with the rioting crowd that he missed his train home. He still talks about Jerry Lee's performance that night as the greatest live show he has ever seen.

The European tour had Jerry Lee very excited. For a country boy from Ferriday, Louisiana, that was like going to another planet. I didn't think you could drive much further than Memphis in any direction without completing a circumnavigation of the planet. Myra insisted that she accompany Jerry Lee. I'm sure that put a wrinkle in the plans that Jerry Lee and Myra's daddy J.W. had in mind. For the biggest part of their lives, they partied and sported with women in tandem. J.W. was just as big a womanizer as Jerry Lee. Hell, this was a major rock 'n' roll band in the heyday of that music. There were women after them around the clock. Europe offered the prospect of a new flock of groupies to choose from. You know, something a little more "exotic." But Myra put the lid on that.

It was only a matter of days into the tour when the press began harping on the cousin/child bride scandal. Jerry finished the tour to protests and shrinking crowds. By the time he returned home, the United States press had picked up the story and were working him over at home. Some folks stood by him, but by and large, the country was just not forgiving when it came to marrying your cousins, at least not when they're only thirteen. Momma had made it pretty damn clear how much she was against it from the start.

Looking back, I'm a pretty liberal person when it comes to bedroom matters, but I believe I'd go berserk right now if my daughter Annie came home at thirteen with a wedding band on, telling me she had married her twenty-year-old first cousin. Somebody would die.

Chapter Five:
The Bottom
Is Up for Me

Jerry Lee and Elvis, contrary to a lot of popular myths, were always friends. They appreciated each other as musicians, entertainers and as people. When they were both young and recording for Sam Phillips, they hung out together riding motorcycles and partying around Memphis. Because of this friendship, we all had a standing invitation to go to Elvis's private showings of movies at the Memphian theater in downtown Memphis. Myra kept telling me that she wanted to introduce me to Elvis since I had never met him. Looking back on it, I know who wanted to go see Elvis — Myra.

Anyway, she finally got me to go with her. As we walked in the lobby of the grand old theater, I immediately saw Elvis on the far side of the room. He was a very courteous gentleman every time I ever saw him, and he walked straight over to us with his hand outstretched to greet us.

Now, being in show business for most of my life, I have

seen a lot of great looking people, male and female. I have to tell you, though, in his prime — early twenties then — this was the single most beautiful person I have ever seen. Face, complexion, teeth, hair, physique, he was incredibly gorgeous. He took my hand and kissed it. I was overcome with his presence and could not even speak. I know my mouth was just hanging wide open. But it was obvious that he was used to this reaction. He just laughed and invited us to come sit with him during the movie. Hell, I haven't got the smallest recollection of what movie we saw, but I'll never live long enough to forget what he looked like then. I'm so glad to have gotten to know him during that period. Our paths would cross numerous times over the years, and he never forgot me and was always gracious.

I saw a lot of Jerry Lee in Elvis and vice versa. That's pretty understandable when you consider the similarities in their upbringing and the relationship they both had with their parents. Not to mention, they were both from the South and great entertainers.

When I was ten years old, Jerry Lee appeared in Monroe, Louisiana, with Johnny Cash. I had been performing in talent shows for years already, but I had never sung at a professional concert. Jerry agreed to let me do one song. I did Marty Robbins' big hit from that time, "A White Sports Coat." I don't know whether it was because I was so young or because I was Jerry Lee's kid sister or what, but I killed the audience. I remember so clearly, and I also remember that it was my first realization that I craved the sort of recognition and response that can be gotten only by performing for a live audience. I was hooked. Hell, I'm still hooked.

From that point on, my focus changed. I had been a fairly

decent student in school up to the ninth grade. Then came math. I decided that anything I had to study that hard held no future for me. My interest and grades fell simultaneously. On the other hand, my interest in the opposite sex was soaring. Thus, I made fairly simple choices. I was no fool. Jerry Lee was making money, having fun and getting laid in spades. Now, *that* was the life I wanted.

There was this one poor little guy named Bobby. I was fourteen, and in heat. My religious upbringing would never allow for unmarried sex at that point in my life. I was still living at home with Momma and the strong influence of the church, even though I was leaning in other directions. Momma had always told me and Frankie Jean that if you had sex with somebody and you weren't married to them, everybody would be able to see it on your face the next day. It would be perfectly obvious to everyone who saw you from then on that you were a tramp, a little whore. What's even more pathetic is that I believed it. Frankie Jean must have too, because she got married the first time when she was twelve years old. My God, the Lewis curse must have been firmly in control of her at an early age.

Bobby thought that my marrying him might be a good thing. I thought marrying anybody might be a good thing. There was also a hidden agenda that played a big part in my decision. Without my parents' permission, I couldn't drop out of high school, and they were not about to allow me to quit school. Jerry Lee was just as upset about my wanting to quit as my parents were. But I hated school, math was getting harder by the day, and I knew that what I really wanted to do was be on the road singing — like Jerry Lee. Bobby represented my ticket to freedom.

It's apparent that no marriage that starts out with such

low expectations has much of a chance. We were together less than two weeks. Even though the marriage quickly folded, it did fulfill all my expectations. In two weeks time, I was out of school, free, and deflowered. I felt that I was finally able to do the things I wanted to. Unfortunately, Bobby didn't fare so well. Within the year, I received a call to inform me that poor Bobby had blown his brains out. Jerry Lee never hesitates to tell me, "Linda, you drove him crazy . . . caused poor Bobby to kill himself." I think Bobby had a lot of problems other than me. I was just one of many.

By 1958, only two years after Phillips first heard him, Jerry Lee's ride at the top of the charts was over. Many of the better known disc jockeys were refusing to play his songs because of the Myra scandal. Dick Clark made a big deal out of the whole thing and refused to play a Jerry Lee Lewis record on any of his programs. Many of the shows that Jerry Lee already had booked started to cancel. Overnight, he went from making $10,000 a night to $200.

In the history of the record industry there have been numerous one-shot artists. There are others that stayed at the top of the charts for years, only to wind up with nothing. An example like Florence Ballard is not rare. She was one of the original Supremes, with ten number-one records, yet she died a few years ago on welfare, leaving a mess of kids in a Detroit housing project.

It would have been nothing unusual for Jerry Lee to drift away into oblivion, working as a mechanic or a factory worker back in Ferriday. His name would have been a trivia question about the history of rock 'n' roll, and that would have been the end of it. As everyone knows, however, that didn't happen.

It's because of the things that Jerry Lee did from that point on that made him great. It's easy to be a big star with people kissing your ass from sunrise to sundown and taking care of all the mundane things in life while stuffing countless dollars in your hand. Who couldn't deal with that? It's having been there and then having to start all over again with a stigma attached to your name that's a nightmare — one that Jerry Lee was now dealing with.

The band was no longer making its rounds on private airplanes or even a bus. Jerry Lee, J.W. Brown, Russell Smith and assorted other part-timers were traveling by car, towing a trailer with our instruments in it. Jerry Lee did not consider quitting for a second. $10,000 or $200 . . . he wasn't playing for the money to start with. He was playing for the love of making music. It was all he ever wanted, and he'll continue till his last breath.

I was begging him constantly to let me travel with him. I can remember promising that I would always ride on the "hump" or the middle seat up front over the transmission. I would do anything if he would just let me go on the road with him. Reluctantly, and seeing that I had pretty well burned all of the other bridges in my world, he agreed to try it for a while to see how it worked out. I was in heaven. At first, Jerry Lee would let me sing a single song at the beginning of the show. After a while, I began to do a number of solos and then duets with Jerry Lee, many of which wound up on his albums from that period.

The crowds were no longer there. We were playing to small, rowdy groups at bars and low-end nightclubs. I remember that some of the early clubs we played at were up north in Chicago. I was young and easily impressed. It didn't strike me then that just because we were having to share dressing rooms with the strippers who went on before and after us meant that the club was not a top-drawer establishment.

The music was decidedly country, even though Jerry Lee always did his big rock 'n' roll hits because the audiences wanted it. The clubs were exactly what you would expect — smoke-filled, loud, dirty and redneck. Jerry's personal problems had even affected his drawing power in these sorts of places, and a lot of nights, the clubs were empty and the club owner lost money. Jerry Lee realized this could kill his reputation on the circuit and leave him nowhere to play. So, if the club had a bad night when he was there, he'd tell the owner that he'd come back again for a small amount of money to make up for it; together they could recoup their loss. This worked for several reasons. First, the people who did come see Jerry Lee loved him and would certainly come see him again and bring others with them. It also meant that the owner would have to rebook him to get the rate reduction. Generally, a repeat show would bring out a good crowd, and slowly, the word got out that Jerry Lee was a good bet for filling up a club.

Another thing that helped was Jerry Lee's country roots. The first time people came to see him, they would generally be expecting a rock 'n' roll act. Once they heard him unwind on a couple of ballads or country standards, they knew there was a lot more to him than boogie woogie. He could do it all.

Myra was staying with Momma in Ferriday at this time. The money was so tight that Jerry Lee shut up the house in Memphis. Again, wherever Momma was, that's where Jerry Lee considered home anyway. In watching Myra's version of Jerry Lee's life in the movie "Great Balls of Fire," it struck me as funny that she thought she even knew what went on. She stayed at home, either in Memphis or Ferriday, ninety percent of the time. She didn't have a clue.

We were up most mornings before the sun was up good, headed for the next gig. This, after staying up most of the night in a honky-tonk in God knows where. Some nights we were booked so far away for the next night's show that we couldn't even check into a motel. We just left one show, got in the car and drove all night to the next one. It never bothered me; in fact, I loved every minute of it. Maybe it was because I was young and eager to see the world or just because I was making music.

Jerry Lee and the band were playing, partying and screwing their eyeballs out. It was funny — Jerry Lee would insist that I was in my room the minute we got to the hotel. He didn't want me to know what was going on, as if that sort of thing could remain hidden. I wasn't stupid. At breakfast, the band would all brag and joke about who they had picked up and laid. I knew from seeing that go on that I would never be a star fucker. I guess those women wanted to be able to say they had screwed Jerry Lee Lewis or one of his band. If they only knew what a non-exclusive group they had become a member of.

Since he started playing on the road, Jerry Lee had always drunk liquor. I think that the grind of all these one-nighters, the pressure from the decline in his career, and the financial problems caused him to start drinking pretty seriously. It's not an easy thing to travel all day, play all night and put on a crisp performance. The traveling by itself takes a big toll on your body. After countless performances and a lifestyle of this sort, Jerry Lee was developing a new legend. The more outrageous his conduct and lifestyle became, the more the audiences loved him.

Before long, the whiskey bottle became flagrantly displayed on the piano in front of Jerry Lee, and he drank heavily during the performance. The worst people in the world to try and remain sober in front of is a bunch of drunks. The clubs we were playing in were redneck havens of the highest order. There were fights almost every night, and every time Jerry Lee took a swig of whiskey, the crowd would roar enthusiastically with approval. He was their kind of people.

I could never understand why people who go out to clubs and bars to hear country music and dance wind up, instead, hitting somebody over the head with a bottle. I've seen more fights than Muhammad Ali. The "Thrilla in Manila" was "Vanilla in Manila" compared to some of the bouts I've seen.

On one night, a drunk in a bar started badmouthing Jerry Lee while he was performing. I think he realized he had crossed the line when he asked Jerry Lee if he was "still fucking your first cousin." That question was answered when Jerry Lee jumped off the stage and into his face. The drunk had apparently been encouraged by the large crowd of similar drunks who were undoubtedly his drinking buddies.

A fight seemed to break out in the entire club at one time. Not to discredit the music-making talents of the band, most of the guys playing with Jerry Lee were pretty damn big and mean, too. A fight didn't scare them in the smallest way. They considered it a fringe benefit of playing in these types of clubs. Good old Cecil produced a set of brass knuckles, and the rest of the guys grabbed whatever was handy. When all was said and done, most of the audience was on the floor. The band was as bloody as an engineer at a train wreck, and Jerry Lee was standing in front of them all with a leg off his piano stool, inviting the next challenger to come forward. The police came and closed the place up. Jerry Lee is not a candy ass.

On another occasion I'll never forget, we were playing in Indianapolis at the Holly O Club. There were some hecklers in the front as usual. Why do they always seat these guys next to the stage? Anyway, this particular group could only be described as "monsters." They were so big that you couldn't see beyond them. Even Jerry Lee and Cecil were having second thoughts about getting into a fracas with this group.

After the show, the band continued to talk about how big they were and how lucky everybody had been that things hadn't gotten any worse. About that time, guess who shows up at the metal door leading from the second floor dressing room. That's right. And, as it turned out, these guys were linemen for the Chicago Bears football team. They had come for a little more ribbing of the "killer."

Cecil met them at the door and tried to convince them to just call it a night. They expressed their firm conviction that they wouldn't be going anywhere until they "damn well felt like it." It got nastier and louder by the moment. Finally, in an attempt to get them to calm down, Jerry Lee went to talk with them. The effort was in vain. They started to call him some pretty foul names and then a swing was taken at Jerry Lee.

Cecil, in an effort to keep him from getting hurt, pushed the one closest to Jerry Lee backwards. He went all the way down the two-story metal steps, taking his two friends with him. The steps did a lot more damage to them than Jerry Lee and Cecil would have ever accomplished. The now battered athletes eventually gathered their composure and started back up the stairs. Cecil quickly shut the metal fire door, and after a few minutes of pounding on it, they gave up and left. To this day, when they tell the story, there's usually a lot of descriptions given like "kickin' their asses" and "runnin' off the Chicago Bears." I never hear them mention anything about stairs or locking the firedoor.

Don't let me give the impression that they always finished on the better end of these little forays. One night on a show with Ray Price, Ray's road manager made a remark about me that upset Jerry Lee, and he got in the guy's face. Jerry Lee was extremely protective of me at that time. There were words but no blows were thrown then. Before the show, after Jerry Lee had already forgotten about it, he was just walking towards the stage when the same guy sucker punched Jerry Lee, splitting his head wide open. When he came to, it was obvious that he needed stitches. The club owner kept saying it was "nothing" and begging Jerry Lee to go on and do the show. He obviously had first-hand experience with the kind of damages a bar can sustain in the case of a "no-show."

Though it's not funny, Jerry Lee has certainly caused his share of these "no-show" club busters over the years. But this night, he *had* to go to the hospital. The band took him to the emergency room, and he had about a half dozen or so stitches put in. Remarkably, he went back to the club and did a show, even though it was a little later than billed.

After we returned, we heard that the guy who had busted Jerry Lee's head had met with the pointed edge of somebody's knife shortly after Jerry Lee left for the hospital. There was some talk that Jerry had "arranged" for it to happen, but I was right beside Jerry Lee the whole time, and he never made any mention of anything like that. Now, that's not to say that an unhappy fan might not have meted out justice on Jerry Lee's behalf.

I mentioned before that our Daddy, Elmo, was a hell raiser and a rounder, and that's true. I've also described my mother as a woman who put God first and everything else second, and that's true also. So, with that in mind, you would naturally assume that Jerry Lee must have gotten his kick-ass attitude from our Daddy. I would have said so myself until one night in Monroe, Louisiana, at the Rendezvous Club.

I was entertaining there as a solo act. I was dating Jerry Lee's long-time band member and friend, Kenny Lovelace. He was there as well as J.W. Brown and Momma. Now, Momma always felt comfortable anywhere she went. She wasn't intimidated by the famous, rich or powerful. She had taken to having an occasional drink and was generally a little looser than she would have been if she hadn't seen a lot of the world outside of Ferriday. She was still the same goodhearted woman, just a little more traveled. Anyway, J.W., who liked to drink and run off at the mouth, decided to go after Momma.

He said, "Aunt Mamie, you know, if it weren't for me, you and your family would still be sharecropping down on Black River."

Now, I know he was only trying to get her dander up, not really ridicule her. Unfortunately, Momma didn't see it that way. She hauled off and hit him with her fist so hard it brought blood. He responded with the sort of profanity one might expect at such a moment, and Momma responded in kind by removing her high-heel shoe and going after him again. If Kenny Lovelace and I had not been there to physically pull her off J.W., I truly believe she would have beat him to death with that shoe. When she got off him, he looked like he had been in a fight with a rabid coon and lost.

Later, when J.W. got back to Memphis, he was at Jerry

Lee and Myra's house and was telling the story to his wife, Jane, and Myra. He was making some unkind remarks about Momma when Jerry Lee heard him. You don't bad-mouth Momma to Jerry Lee. He went over to the three of them and said, "You just shut the hell up and get out of my house. I don't know who you people think you are. Myra, I married you at thirteen and you weren't a virgin, and J.W., I might just have to tell your wife here about all the whores you've been with when you're on the road."

Believe it or not, these same two got into it one night at Lynn Anderson's Nashville estate. Lynn's husband, Glen Sutton, had written "What's Made Milwaukee Famous," a big hit for Jerry Lee. To celebrate the song's success, Lynn had invited Jerry Lee and the band to her house for a pretty upscale party. There were a number of famous guests in attendance, and I'm sure Lynn was not expecting J.W. and Kenny to get into a brawl.

Now, I don't know who said what to whom. I do know that if I had to bet on how it got started, I'd put my money on J.W. running off at the mouth again. No matter how it started, before long, it was a full-fledged, knock-down-drag-out affair. They tumbled into the foyer and crashed into this extremely expensive, antique crystal lamp that Lynn had purchased in Europe. The lamp was dead on arrival of Kenny and J.W. They continued until they were physically separated by Jerry Lee and the rest of the guests. Needless to say, after that, we were never on the "A" list for parties around the Music City. I'm sure it never bothered our entourage, as our entire life was a continual party.

Jerry Lee's behavior, even though expected from him, was in direct contrast to what was expected from the other acts, generally country headliners that we often traveled with. We worked with practically every major country star over the years. Faron Young was one of Jerry Lee's running mates. He had a lot of the same interests — drinking, women and partying. They painted a lot of towns red between the two of them.

On the other end of the spectrum were the country stars who emphasized traditional family values and wholesome entertainment. Jerry Lee offered great entertainment but definitely did not try and present a wholesome image. He was the proverbial singer in a bottle.

Connie Smith was the classic example. We had been traveling with a big-time country show that was hot during the early sixties. Other headliners were Johnny Cash, Mother Maybelle Carter and Kitty Wells. Connie Smith had a monster hit with "Once a Day." Shortly thereafter, she also had a major religious conversion and had practically become a Tennessee big-haired version of Mother Teresa. We were not her cup of tea. She went on before us, and she knew who the crowd was there to see. It sure wasn't her. She opened up her act by addressing the audience.

"I just want you people to know that I do not agree with anything that the Lewis family stands for. I'm nothing like them. I just happened to be on the same show and that's all. I totally disagree with their lifestyle, their music and everything they do." That said, she sang the only decent hit she ever had and undoubtedly ever will have.

When Jerry Lee took the stage, he totally ignored everything she had said. He put on an unbelievable show, ending with him taking off his drenching wet shirt and leaving the stage to a standing ovation. As he passed by Mother Maybelle Carter and Kitty Wells, they were looking at him in obvious disgust. He looked them right in the eye, took his ringing wet, sweaty shirt and threw it directly into their faces. He said, "Now, what do you think about that?" They hated us. I know where they were coming from. We were completely outrageous.

A lot of the folks we traveled with, though country stars, were wonderful people, and we became close friends. A couple of my favorites were George Jones and Tammy Wynette. Now, mixing George Jones and Jerry Lee Lewis together was probably not a good idea. George, like Jerry Lee, is best known in country for his ballads, songs like "He Stopped Loving Her Today" or "The Grand Tour." But George is one of the original country rockers. If you have seen one his shows, you know what I'm talking about. He shares a lot of similarities with Jerry Lee, the smallest of which is not his attraction to the bottle and fast women. We were close with George Jones and Tammy Wynette when they were just starting to see each other. There was one night when George and Jerry Lee got so wasted that they both missed their spots on different shows the following night.

Several supposed "stars" were particularly offensive to either Jerry Lee or me. On one particular tour, Johnny Rivers was a headliner and went out of his way to be an asshole to Jerry Lee. He considered Jerry Lee to be an over-the-hill "has-been" and himself to be a really big star. Every time he talked with Jerry Lee, it was condescending, as he made it very apparent how he felt. They finally got into an argument in Jerry Lee's dressing room. Jerry Lee was screwing in a light over the mirror, and after he heard all he wanted, he told Johnny Rivers that if he didn't shut up and get the hell out of his dressing room, he would be leaving with that light bulb up his ass. He left.

On one of the Shindig tours, when I was appearing solo,

a young and not-so-famous Cher was booked. The place we were in was tiny without a lot of dressing rooms. They had put Cher and me in the same dressing room. She walked in, took one look at country me, and said, "I'm not sharing a dressing room with anybody!" She had an attitude that wouldn't quit. Even after she got to be a huge star, I could always see that in her whenever I saw her on a show. She was definitely not a nice lady.

Chapter Six:
So We're *a* Little Bit Different

Momma and Daddy were no longer living in Ridgecrest. Daddy had always loved farming, and during the good times, Jerry Lee had bought him a farm in the Indian Village, which is just outside of Clayton, Louisiana. Daddy was not farming for a living — he was a gentleman farmer. I think not having to work so hard became a problem for him. Daddy was drinking and running around on Momma. She knew it and stood by him, but the handwriting was on the wall.

Whenever we didn't have a show, we were home. And, Jerry Lee never missed a funeral. If a close friend or family member passed away, our whole family would show up for the service. This included Mickey Gilley and Jimmy Swaggart. Jimmy would almost always preside over the service. He never missed an opportunity to encourage and prod Jerry Lee to come back to the church, to cast aside his interests in the Devil's music and lifestyle.

I gotta admit, Jimmy can cast a spell from the pulpit. And Jerry Lee and Mickey have a weak spot when they hear the call. It's almost like a scene from an Abbott and Costello comedy. Jimmy starts singing "Come home . . . come home . . . yee who are weary . . . come home. . . ." The choir would join in a building crescendo, the congregation would start raising their hands and encouraging their lost children. Lord, this was great theater.

And what singing! How many churches with a membership of around fifty would have three best-selling recording artists to sing along with them? They, as much as anybody in the congregation, would get caught up in the spirit. And there they would go, falling all over the altar, confessing their sins, asking for forgiveness and vowing to walk the straight and narrow. At least early on, it used to make Momma feel better to see that Jerry Lee still had this inside of him.

But, as they say, the flesh is weak. It would generally take Jerry Lee at least four full hours after the ceremony to find a bottle and a woman. Still, it was this constant battle inside of him that gave his voice that feeling of conviction and sincerity that make his ballads so emotional. You can tell in his voice that the feeling is real . . . he's been there.

It was about this time, with Jerry Lee struggling to keep enough money coming in to provide for Momma and Daddy, and to keep the band on the road, that Momma decided Jerry Lee should buy a car for Jimmy. She was as active as ever in the church, and Jimmy was doing the Lord's work. Jerry Lee would never argue with Momma. If she wanted him to buy Jimmy Swaggart a car, he would buy him one, and so he did. Hell, I would like to have half the money Jerry Lee has spent on cars for other people in his lifetime. I'll bet he's given more of them away than Elvis ever thought of. As long as Momma was alive, he would buy her a new Cadillac every year. This included all of the years when he could barely afford a decent car for the band to travel in.

I remember one year, we were so tight that all he could afford to buy Momma was an Oldsmobile Starfire. It was a fine car, but not a new Fleetwood. It was a sign to her that Jerry Lee must really have fallen on hard times. He also kept Momma a full-time maid and housekeeper, right up till she died. If Momma wanted it, Jerry Lee bought it for her.

I'll never forget one time when Jerry Lee had been trying to scrape together enough money to buy himself a new Cadillac. He had recently taken a "Pauper's Vow." That's very similar to what declaring bankruptcy is today. Needless to say, he didn't have much money and no credit. For that reason, he had to set aside cash to buy a car. Jerry Lee always loved Cadillacs. They were an indication that you were doing well back then, and it's always been important to entertainers to appear that they were doing great, even if they weren't. Nobody wants to pay to watch somebody who couldn't afford to attend his own show if he had to pay.

So, Jerry Lee had saved up the money and finally bought this beautiful, though somewhat gaudy, red Caddy. It had gold trim and a Landau top. It was a show business car — too tacky for just anybody to ride up and down the street in. It was the kind of car that if you saw it coming, you'd say, "Who the hell is that?" Jerry Lee loved that car.

Well, Momma had been visiting with Jerry Lee in Memphis. Just before her bedtime, she came into the living room where Jerry Lee and I were sitting, watching television. She matter-of-factly said, "Jerry Lee, I'll be heading back to Ferriday in the morning, and I'm thinking I might like to drive that red Cadillac."

Jerry Lee quickly responded, "That's fine, Momma. If you want to drive my car home, you just go right ahead and take it."

The next morning, we helped Momma pack up the car and kissed her goodbye. As she drove off, a pathetic Jerry Lee, hands in his pockets, turned to me with the saddest look on his face and said, "Linda Gail, that's the last I'll ever see of that car." It was. Momma loved it and kept it till it was time for her new one.

To tell you the truth, for what our folks had to go through, the poverty and all while they were raising us, I still think they deserved all the spoiling that Jerry Lee was willing to give them. I'm sure he doesn't regret one dime he ever gave to either of them.

During this "down" time in Jerry Lee's career, he never quit trying to record another hit record. Some of his best cuts were recorded, but the problem was strictly no airplay. Even Judd Phillips, who undoubtedly invented payola, could not get the jocks to play Jerry Lee's songs. He had been effectively cut off from the mainstream of the music scene of that period. Shelby Singleton had bought all of Jerry Lee's recordings from Sam Phillips, and Jerry continued to go into the studio and search for a way to get another hit. It had been more than ten years since Jerry Lee had been at the top of the charts. And ten years on the road is a lifetime.

Through sheer willpower and talent, Jerry Lee had established himself among the club owners throughout the country as somebody who could put on a show and fill a house. He had steadily worked his way back up the ladder to where he was making a good living. We had gone from a single old Cadillac for the entire band, to a tour bus and a new Caddy for Jerry Lee and me.

Two other big factors in the renewed interest in Jerry Lee were the TV show "Shindig" and the play "Catch My Soul" which was a rock 'n' roll version of the famous Shakespearean play, "Othello" which Jerry Lee did in Los Angeles. He played the part of Iago and got rave reviews. He was a huge draw for both shows and the exposure helped draw crowds to his own appearances.

I've never mentioned it before, but I was offered the chance to play Desdemona in the play, and I wanted to do it. But Jerry Lee wouldn't hear of it because I would have had to kiss William Marshall, the black actor who played Othello. He was handsome and a great guy. I had no problems with it, but Jerry Lee was the boss. He was never overtly prejudiced towards black people, which is pretty amazing when you consider our background and where we were raised. As a matter of fact, he loved old Mr. Haney who used to let him sneak into his club at night to listen to the great R&B acts that came to town. Another great black performer, Fats Domino, was always one of Jerry Lee's best friends. He just wasn't advanced enough to have his baby sister bearing down on a black man. Hell, this guy was a Rhodes Scholar and a monk compared to a lot of the guys I'd already spent time with in the back seat of the Caddy.

Another good thing came from the "Shindig" show. The host, a wonderful man named Jack Good, thought I had talent and let me do solos on the nationally broadcast show. I did "The Girl from Wolverton Mountain" and "Thanks a

Lot." He was very kind to me and encouraged me to pursue a solo career. He asked me to go solo on his Elvis tribute show later, which Jerry Lee insisted I do. I sang "Crying in the Chapel" and "Don't Be Cruel," and it went over well with the producer and the audience. I was invited to go on the "Shindig" national tour, which I jumped on.

By this time, I was also having an affair with the producer of the show. Seems like singing and screwing always went together in my life. I was only seventeen at the time, and I think that this brief stint as a solo act planted the seeds for my desire to see what I could do on my own years later. I wasn't particularly ambitious back then. I was still thrilled to be traveling with my brother. I loved him as much as a sister could a brother, and I respected all that he had done for our family.

Along with the increased attention Jerry Lee was attracting came some realization by record company execs that money could be made by putting out some decent records and promoting them. And money is the name of the business. Hell, even Sam Phillips, when he realized what a predicament Jerry Lee was in over the marriage with Myra, had put out a record making fun of the whole incident, "The Return of Jerry Lee." He did this to make a few bucks out of the misfortunes of a man who trusted him and had made him millions of dollars. Incidentally, I think it's worth mentioning right here that as word of this book got out, Jerry Phillips, Sam's son, called me and asked me if I was "willing to sell my soul for a few lousy bucks?" I had to say that I couldn't understand their concern when Sam had been willing to sell souls for money, especially other people's souls. And not for just a few bucks. He had made a killing off Jerry Lee, and ten years after the fact, he still had not paid Jerry

Lee a cent in royalties beyond the original $40,000 he had given him right after he hit big. Hell, if I was just looking to throw tales around to make money, I'd have certainly not have forgotten to mention the fact that Judd Phillips and I had an affair when I was fourteen years old and he was a middle-aged promoter. But, I didn't do it . . . at least not until I got pissed off remembering how bad Sam Phillips had fucked over Jerry Lee. And besides, I seduced him. He was a nice guy and very handsome.

Jerry Lee loved Judd Phillips and Judd always took Jerry Lee's side, even when the arguments were with his brother. One day, just a few years ago, we were at Jerry Lee's house in Memphis, and he started reminiscing about the old days. Jerry got on the subject of Judd, and he said, "One thing I can say for Judd that I can't about any other man I ever knew, he was always faithful to his wife." I almost choked on my drink. I never told him, or anyone until now, what had happened between me and Judd.

While we're talking about Sam and money . . . let me tell this story. I laugh out loud everytime I think about it. Jerry Lee had been given a beautiful, very large and ferocious-looking guard dog by a fan. It was a German shepherd and responded to verbal commands spoken in German. Jerry Lee took delight in scaring people by making it growl at them. Now, it would also attack if given the command, but that was something Jerry Lee wouldn't do unless he felt he was truly in danger. Nevertheless, on command, this magnificent animal would bare his mouth full of razor-sharp teeth and give the most bloodcurdling growl while staring his intend-ed victim in the eyes.

Jerry Lee was broke . . . as usual. It had been years since he had made decent money. Sam had not paid him his royalties, and he was obviously rolling in Jerry Lee bucks. Jerry Lee was high as a Georgia pine and pissed off about not having enough money for a new Caddy. So he loaded the dog into the car and went off to Sam's. He ran into Judd Phillips first, who accompanied him to Sam's office. Sam, not knowing what was up, welcomed him as usual, like his long-lost prodigal son. Jerry Lee was not amused.

After they went into Sam's office, Jerry Lee had the dog sit down right beside him and then said, "Sam, I want my fucking money, and if you don't give it to me, I'm just gonna have to have my dog here chew your ass up!" Jerry gave the growl order to the dog, and he produced the appropriate life-threatening sounds while looking Sam Phillips right in the face. Now Judd, who always supported Jerry Lee, encouraged him to let the animal have at Sam. "Let him go, Jerry Lee. Let him eat his ass up. Let him go, Jerry Lee. Go get him boy . . . go eat him up."

Sam, without so much as a blink, took a deep breath, a long pause, and replied, "Jerry Lee, I love you like a son and you're the most talented musician I've ever met. However, there's only thing I love more than you, and that's money. I love it and I ain't giving you a fucking penny. So, you go ahead and let that dog have at me if you want to, but you ain't getting a cent. Besides, you'd just piss it away like you did the money I already gave you."

Jerry Lee would never have let the dog kill Sam. He actually loved the man and never forgot that he had given him the chance to make records when everybody else had passed on him. Never mind the fact that he had kept the lion's share of Jerry Lee's success for himself. Not until this day has Jerry Lee made any effort to sue him. And he no doubt wouldn't be doing it now if it weren't for his wife, Kerrie. Hell, she and Sam should have gotten married. The only thing she ever loved about Jerry Lee was his money, too! She has apparently begun the steps required to attempt to collect the royalties from Jerry Lee's records that Sam has managed to keep to himself all these years. From all the horror stories I've heard from other "stars" of that period, a sharp lawyer could make billions collecting the royalties the producers have kept while paying out nothing in royalties.

I remember Jerry Lee fussing to me one time about it, and he remarked, "You know, Linda Gail, how can those bastards have the nerve to present me with all these fucking gold records and no money?" When you think about it, it is kind of the ultimate slap in the face to a performer. "Here's something shiny you can hang on your wall. We'll hang onto the dirty old money."

Chapter Seven:
The Killer
Returns

Jerry Lee had gone from Sun Records to Shelby Singleton at Mercury Records in fairly short order. He had been recording with no commercial success worth mentioning for almost ten years. Shelby worked as Jerry Lee's producer when he was first signed to Mercury. When Shelby left Mercury, one of the labels he started after buying the Sun catalogs was Sun International. He released some of Jerry's biggest country hits that Sun had produced in 1963. But even though they were recorded before Jerry left Sun, they didn't hit the charts until after Jerry Lee's hits started coming out on Smash (Mercury). It's interesting that after Jerry Lee's recording career started to get hot again, Shelby had several big hits off records that Jerry Lee had cut years earlier that didn't sell. Again, recognition and increased bookings for larger dollars were all Jerry Lee got out of the record sales. Some of these albums are still being released successfully today, and even national television commercials are using some of the cuts. Boy, these guys have nerve.

Jerry Lee started with Mercury around 1963, and his records were being produced there by the legendary country music personality Jerry Kennedy. But after a couple of lackluster years, Mercury had made the decision to drop Jerry Lee, and undoubtedly this would have been the final nail in the coffin of Jerry Lee's recording career. That was when Eddie Kilroy came into the picture. He loved Jerry Lee's ability to fill a ballad with soul and emotion. He asked for permission to cut one record with Jerry Lee, kind of a last-ditch effort to salvage him for the label. Reluctantly, they agreed.

Eddie spent a great deal of time trying to find just the right song for Jerry Lee. Finally he found it. Eddie told Jerry Lee that the only way he would do it was for Jerry Lee to let him dictate how it was put together, the arrangement and style. Jerry Lee, knowing that he desperately needed a hit and that nothing else was working, agreed. He produced the record "Another Place, Another Time," which became Jerry Lee's first major hit in ten years.

Not too remarkably, it was a country hit, establishing Jerry Lee firmly in that area. This record was a major shot in the arm to Jerry Lee's concerts and increased the demand for additional records, which he was only too delighted to record. A series of terrific country ballads followed and Jerry Lee, the rock 'n' roller who could sing country, had been reborn as Jerry Lee the country, bar, ballad master who could also sing rock 'n' roll. In most ways, this was a much better fit for what Jerry Lee liked to do musically. Needless to say, Jerry Lee's appearance price shot right back up to $10,000 a night, plus.

By sheer determination and will power, Jerry Lee had

climbed back to his rightful stature in the music business. His relentless touring for years at the $200-a-night clubs, his forays into television and plays, and now at last, a string of new hit records had put him back on the top. And how was Eddie Kilroy rewarded for salvaging a ruined career and a Mercury artist who wasn't making them any money? He was immediately fired. He had embarrassed Jerry Kennedy and the powers that be at Mercury, not to mention putting Jerry Lee in a position to make demands of the label — something they did not want to have to tolerate.

For the band and our life on the road, it meant that we had graduated from one car and a U-Haul trailer to a bus and limousine, to airplanes and the red carpet. It was well deserved after ten years of grueling one-night stands and all-day drives to the next gig. The band and I were thrilled to be flying instead of driving. There were a few shortcomings with the planes we had. They were never brand-new, and they were generally not the luxury models. They were rather interesting in one regard. Because they had all been remodeled to accommodate bands, they always had a bar on them. Yet, as funny as it may seem, they never had a bathroom. In fact, because there was no toilet on the first couple we flew, we had to use a Coke bottle to take a pee. Who in their right mind would put in a beer keg and no place to take a leak, 10,000 feet in the air? We all joked about it. Hell, we were all so high most of the time, we'd have taken a leak off the wing if somebody had thought of it.

Jerry Lee had a very interesting relationship with airplanes. He seemed to be able to feel when the plane was not performing up to snuff. He would have a feeling come over him and suddenly, without logical explanation, he would demand that the plane be replaced. Initially there was a lot of resistance to making such an expensive switch without any logical reason, especially when the pilots and the people servicing the planes said they were in perfect condition. They should have known better than to argue with Jerry Lee when his mind was made up. The plane went or Jerry Lee didn't.

The first time this occurred, the plane was an old DC-3. It had been a reliable, stout plane that had carried us across the country many, many times. Jerry Lee wouldn't get back on it, so it had to be sold. It was sold to the famous '50s rock 'n' roll star Ricky Nelson. Within a month, the plane crashed, killing Nelson and his band. From then on out, if this feeling came back over Jerry Lee, he would refuse to step back on the plane that was the source of this emotion.

The replacement for the ill-fated DC-3 was a Convair. It was a large prop plane, formerly used as an airliner but now converted to a special charter plane for such groups as Jerry Lee's band. Again, we all felt very safe and comfortable for several years. None of us noticed any difference in the plane from one trip to the next. Out of the blue, in the middle of a trip, Jerry Lee once again had that uneasy feeling come over him. As soon as we landed, he called his management people and told them to get him another plane, right then. Knowing his history in these matters, they complied, this time without argument. The plane was sold to the rock band Lynyrd Skynyrd. Several of its members died when it crashed shortly thereafter.

Believe it or not, it happened a third time with a Jet Commander that Jerry Lee had been using. Again, the same feeling, the same change of planes and this time, thank God, no band was on board when it crashed. Even the pilot lived to say that the plane had crashed for no apparent reason. It just decided to fall out of the sky and did. They had argued in support of the Jet Commander strongly to no avail. After it crashed, I asked the pilot, "If the entire band had been on board, with a full tank of fuel and all of our equipment, could the plane have survived this crash?" He replied that had that scenario occurred, we would have all been killed.

I have no explanations for how Jerry Lee was able to determine that it was time to get away from these particular planes. I just know that he did it, and I'm here today because of his ability to feel that something was wrong.

With these new successes in his career, there was an equally dramatic change in Jerry Lee's personal life. Throughout the "down years" Jerry Lee had suffered a number of tragedies. First, there was a continuing succession of failed marriages. There had been Dorothy, Jane and Myra. Myra and Jerry Lee stayed married for more than ten years and had a son whom they named after the television star Steve Allen, who had given Jerry Lee the first big break on his show. Steve Allen Lewis drowned when he was only three years old. He was playing outside with the water hose, and Myra took her eyes off him for only a couple of minutes. He apparently got tangled in the hose and fell into the pool. When she found him in the water, it was too late. It was a disastrous blow to Jerry Lee. His Holiness Church upbringing was in the back of his mind always, and he believed that his child had been taken from him as punishment for his lifestyle.

Jerry Lee would go through periods of depression and then back to his religious roots. Many times, he'd go home to the church in Ferriday, confess his sins to the world, repent and start all over again by the end of the week — drinking, running around and all the other activities associated with his sinful life on the road.

Throughout all of these years while Jerry Lee was on the

road, our cousin Jimmy Swaggart was still preaching and slowly developing his own legendary status as a filled-with-the-spirit evangelist. And he never hesitated to barbecue Jerry Lee from the pulpit. I'm not saying that he used Jerry Lee as a famous name that he could associate with his own to promote his career, but it sure didn't hurt. His preaching circuit had become a stepping stone for his ministry, very much the same tool as Jerry Lee's small club circuit had been for his career. They were each advancing to different destinations using the same path. Only time would reveal that their destinations weren't all that far apart.

Momma and Daddy separated and divorced in 1963 after Momma had put up with Daddy's running around for years. She still loved him and I know he always loved her, right up till the day each one of them died. The final straw between them was broken when Myra ratted on Daddy to Momma, and she couldn't ignore it any longer. Daddy had been drinking and running around ever since Jerry first hit the charts. I guess Jerry Lee's success ruined Daddy's life, too. He was a perfect example of idle hands being the Devil's tool.

After Momma died, Daddy was living in a small house on Jerry Lee's estate in Memphis. It's actually in Nesbit, Mississippi, which is almost a suburb of Memphis. Anyway, Charlotte (Pumpkin) and her mother, Jo Ann, were both living there at that time, and Jerry Lee claimed to be sleeping with both of them. For some reason, they got it in their heads that Daddy shouldn't be using the washer and dryer in their house.

Later that evening, Jerry Lee was on tour when he got a call from the Sheriff's Department back home. "Mr. Lewis, listen, your father has had an argument with your wife and her mother. They've locked themselves in the house and they have called us saying he was breaking down the doors with an axe and saying he's going to chop them up in little pieces. He's already knocked down one door with the axe. What do you want us to do?"

Jerry Lee was stunned. "Well, for God's sake, don't let him kill them. Just wait till he gets through the next door. If he keeps on going, just do what it takes to subdue him but please don't haul him off to jail." Of course, he didn't kill them, but more and more I saw a side of him that could explain where Jerry Lee and Frankie Jean got those ways.

Momma and Daddy are both dead, Momma in 1972 and Daddy six years later. I can say with certainty that neither Jerry Lee nor myself ever got over losing them. Momma had been the light of Jerry Lee's life, and her loss sent him back into depression and the bottle in a big way. She died of cancer and it wasn't a fast death. He could hardly bring himself to visit her during her final days because it upset him so terribly.

Jerry Lee was now drinking a tremendous amount and entertaining the continually present bimbos in ever-increasing numbers. His legend was also growing. There's nothing quite like the return of a star to his former status to secure a permanent spot in entertainment history. Jerry Lee had become an icon to many in rock 'n' roll. The sixties had brought with them the "British Invasion," a large number of English rock 'n' roll acts that were put into high gear with the success of the Beatles. Jerry Lee had nothing kind to say about these shaggy-headed sissies that knocked him and numerous others out of the limelight in the United States. His usual description of them was, "those long-haired mutherfuckers!" Any time their name was mentioned or their records were played, the same response could be heard anywhere within shouting distance.

We were appearing in Los Angeles at the Roxie. The show was sold out, and Jerry Lee killed the audience, as usual. After the show, we were in his dressing room backstage. He was pretty well drained and not really up to visitors, but Jerry Lee has always made time for his fans. I've seen him many nights when I knew he was not only feeling horrible, but after some of the major misfortunes that had been occurring in his life he wasn't emotionally up to even doing the shows. This was one of those times. He was not in a mood to take any visitors. He had left word with the show security and the band to please just let him rest a while. I was talking with him, trying to get him to take a break, maybe go back to Ferriday and just cool off.

There was a knock on the dressing room door, and I looked towards Jerry Lee to see if he wanted me to answer it. "Are you gonna see who's at the door or not, Linda Gail?" He didn't look well and I hesitated for a while. "Linda Gail, are you going to open the door?"

I walked over and pulled it open. There was this small, oriental looking woman wearing dark glasses — another fan, I presumed. She stepped aside and let a friend who was standing behind her come in ahead of her. It didn't take me but seconds to recognize John Lennon. He smiled and asked if they could come in to meet Jerry Lee. I was almost too dumbfounded to speak . . . this was the last person I expected to show up. There was also the promise of this being a rather awkward moment, given Jerry Lee's feelings towards the British rock groups and all of the public comments he had made.

As they walked into the room, I tried to warn Jerry Lee,

to give him a chance to gather himself. "Why, Jerry Lee, look who's here to see you — John Lennon." Now, Jerry Lee would probably not do a double take if he were seated at the Last Supper, but what happened next left even him speechless. John Lennon bent down, got on his hands and knees and crawled across the room to where Jerry Lee was seated. Without saying a word, he reached out, grabbed Jerry Lee's foot on his typically crossed leg, and kissed it! "Jerry Lee," he said, "I just wanted to meet you and tell you what an inspiration your music was for me. Whenever you hear the Beatles sing, you should realize what a large influence you had on the whole group."

Jerry Lee was speechless. He could barely get out "Thank you, John . . . Thank you." In just a matter of a moment, John and Yoko Ono, who I hadn't heard of at that time, left the room. Well, from that day on you might be able to get away with an off-color comment about British rock bands in general or the British Invasion, but don't you dare bad-mouth the Beatles to Jerry Lee. They had paid him respect for his talent and that meant far more to him than any record sales they may have taken away from him.

That was not the end of strange occurrences that evening. I was walking backstage by myself a short while later and saw a mop of white hair and a boney, wire-jawed face I recognized instantly. It was Rod Stewart. I walked over to him and introduced myself. He was very cordial, and I asked him if he wanted to meet Jerry Lee. Now, I'm not exaggerating at all when I say that Rod Stewart was afraid to go to Jerry Lee's dressing room. He had heard a lot of the wild comments that Jerry Lee had made, and he was not willing to risk a confrontation, even though I assured him that Jerry Lee would be a very proper gentleman and very glad to meet him. He still refused but, he did take the time to ask me if I wanted to go out with him that evening.

I have to admit, at that time in my life, I was very striking looking with long dark hair, a healthy shape and a fondness for my skin-tight gold lame' skirt. It appeared to be practically spray painted on me, and I could barely walk in it. Now, I will also admit that I did avail myself of a large number of the better, more attractive offers that were placed before me during those days. However, there was a small sticking point that evening. I was with a man I would ultimately have one of the great loves of my life with, a physician named Hall Worthington. We never married, but our relationship was always special, and we are still very close today.

There was another consideration I thought worthy of mentioning to him also. "Why, Rod, you already have three women with you tonight. I'm not very good at sharing."

He smiled with those brilliant white choppers and replied, "Linda Gail, if you'll go out with me, I'll get rid of these young ladies, and we'll have a very special evening." I still declined, but in looking back over the offer today, it makes me get a little flushed when I see him singing and getting down. He's got to be one of the sexiest guys ever.

There was another especially memorable evening where we had a brush with a remarkable talent. We were doing a show in a small North Carolina town. There was a noisy crowd there, before, during and after the show. It was definitely a Pabst Blue Ribbon affair. Early in the evening, before we went on, a security guard backstage was keeping the fans out. They could have literally walked up on the stage and to the dressing rooms if it weren't for the security officers. At the front of the group was a particularly ratty looking young woman, with stringy black hair down the middle of her back and covering a lot of her face. She was very loud and demanded to be allowed backstage. She looked familiar but I thought nothing more about her as I went to the dressing room.

Shortly into the show, we were all on stage, Jerry Lee at the piano rocking away and me and the band were providing the backup harmony. Out of the blue, this same, dirty looking woman with a large bag over her shoulder came up on the stage. Apparently a lot of the people in the audience recognized her before we did, as many of them starting screaming and egging her on. She marched straight over to Jerry Lee and sat down beside him on the piano bench. She reached deep into her purse and retrieved a fifth of Southern Comfort and took a long swallow before placing it on the piano in front of her. Jerry Lee didn't know her from Adam, and after she started singing along with him, he got up, mike in hand, and walked over to me while he continued to sing.

"Who the fuck is that?" was the best he could muster. It was absolutely hilarious by this time. The young woman was playing his piano, and he was trying to ignore her. I knew by now who she was and replied, "That's Janis Joplin."

"Who?" Jerry responded.

"You know, "'Me and Bobby McGee.'"

"She's a damn mess is what she is."

Anyway, she remained for the entire show, sitting and drinking, singing along when she wanted and getting more and more drunk as the evening wore on. It took its toll on Jerry Lee as he did not like anybody disrupting his performance, not even Janis Joplin. She accompanied Jerry Lee backstage to his dressing room after the show. Things began to actually go down hill even farther there.

Normally, after a country show, there would be a number of guests allowed into the dressing room to meet Jerry Lee, if he was up to it. He valued these meetings, generally with disc jockeys, radio station owners or trade newspapers. They would often bring their families, friends and children with them. This was one of those nights.

Janis seated herself next to Jerry Lee while the guests were escorted in. I'm sure Jerry Lee just hoped she would listen and be respectful, as he would have done, but that did not happen. To just about every question, she would respond with a nonsensical answer that generally contained some form of the word *fuck*. As best I can remember, there was "motherfucker," singular and plural numerous times, "No fuck?" addressed as a question, and the answer repeatedly, "Fuckin' A", as well as several others I just can't recall. Jerry Lee was at first embarrassed (that ain't easy to do), and then he got pissed.

In short order, he had her removed, and not too far down the road, she removed herself from this world. She was a great talent, but a very, very, troubled young woman.

Church where Jerry Lee, Mickey, and Jimmy all grew up,
Ferriday First Assembly of God.

Mamie, Jerry Lee, Frankie Jean, Linda Gail,
and Elmo in Black River, around 1954.

Frankie Jean's teenage wedding.
(l. to r.) Elmo holding Jerry Lee Jr., Mamie, Linda Gail, Frankie Jean, Johnny Frank, Jane, and Jerry Lee.

Linda Gail playing the accordion that Jerry Lee bought her.

Linda Gail playing the piano in the new house
that Jerry Lee bought for the family.

Jerry Lee and Mamie at the first house
he bought her in Ridgecrest, Ferriday.

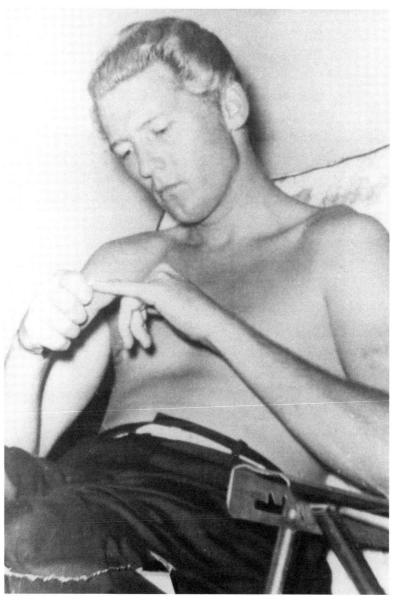

Jerry Lee in California at a friend's home, about 1964.

Myra, Jerry Lee Jr., and baby Steve Allen,
who was born in Ferriday at Concordia Parish Hospital.

Jerry Lee Jr., Jerry Lee, and Mamie.

Linda Gail and Jerry Lee on the road in the 60s.

Linda Gail, age 14, at her wedding to Bobby Goga.

Jimmy Lee Swaggart and Jerry Lee.

Jerry Lee and Linda Gail at Jerry Lee's birthday party at the
Thunderbird Club in Memphis, 1975.

Jerry Lee in concert in Sweden.

Jerry Lee and Linda Gail.

Kerrie and Jerry Lee's wedding, around 1985.

Kerrie, Jerry Lee's wife.

Jerry Lee and Linda Gail on Jerry's birthday, September 1995.

Chapter Eight:
The Bottom Side of the Top

It's hard for me to sit here today and criticize anybody who did drugs or liquor back then. After Momma died, Jerry Lee and I were both on drugs most of the time. Jerry Lee was addicted to the hardcore prescription stuff like Demerol, and I had a passion for Quaaludes. We were both headed down a dead-end road and running wide open.

It's amazing that physicians, men who can honestly make a handsome living and at some point in their lives thought enough about helping people to undergo the struggle that's required to finish medical school, would knowingly write prescriptions for addicts. Without their help, I truly believe that Jerry Lee would never have had a drug problem. Alcohol, yes — he still liked the bottle and abused it heavily.

But the drugs are what started to kill him, and me.

Good old Doctor Nick (short for Nicopolous) was a leading participant in furnishing drugs for Jerry Lee. How this guy has avoided prison all these years still amazes me. He was implicated so deeply in Elvis' death that he should be doing gratis prostrate exams at the "Big House" by any reasonable account.

During this time of renewed fame and great money, the Jerry Lee Lewis show should have been called "The Highest Show on Earth." On stage and off, the excesses were to the point of obscenity. There was sex, liquor, drugs, guns . . . oh, yes, Jerry Lee always loved guns. They were toys that have caused him a great deal of problems. Several instances come to mind.

The first involved a young woman that Jerry Lee had become especially fond of for her unique ability to "suck the chrome off a bumper hitch." Well, her husband, who just happened to be a neighbor, had been alerted to the fact that she was performing this miraculous feat at Jerry Lee's house at that moment. He lost no time in paying a visit. He burst into the bedroom where this show was underway and demanded that the curtain be drawn and the feature performance be brought to a close, immediately.

He began to get a little too abusive, by Jerry Lee's account of the incident. So Jerry Lee pulled out his much loved submachine gun, which he kept fully loaded in the bedroom (doesn't everyone?) and sprayed the air all around his neighbor, who very quickly lost interest in retrieving his shapely vacuum of a wife. Fortunately, he wasn't hit by a bullet. Jerry Lee swears he shot over his head just to scare him off. Some folks have suggested that one experience with a submachine gun when it fires would convince you that aiming it is not all that precise a science. Another incident did not end quite so peacefully or without injuries.

A friend of Jerry Lee's had given him a very powerful .357 Magnum pistol. Jerry Lee kept it loaded and enjoyed playing with it a great deal, even when he was too stoned to safely operate a toothbrush. Butch Owens played the bass in Jerry Lee's band. He was a decent enough guy; no different from a dozen others that Jerry Lee had in the band over the years. They were in between gigs, and Jerry Lee had him and several other band members over to his house in Memphis.

This evening, Jerry Lee was fairly fried and playing with his new weapon. Butch Owens made the mistake of getting him going, and Jerry Lee somehow discharged the gun into Butch's chest. Now, a .357 Magnum blasts a huge hole in a person, and this was a close-range shot, point blank into him. Butch fell to the floor immediately, and Jerry Lee dropped the gun. He swears to this day he never meant for the gun to go off, and apparently the authorities agreed with him because he was never charged with a crime for the shooting. Butch almost died on the floor of the living room. A helicopter was flown in and he just barely made it to the trauma unit, which saved him.

About two weeks after the shooting, Jerry Lee and the band had to go back on the road. Cecil Harrelson, who was acting as a road manager then, asked Jerry Lee who he wanted to get to fill in for Butch till he got well. Jerry Lee, high again, replied, "Until he gets well? Hell, he ain't never gonna be well enough to play the bass for me again. Fire his ass!"

I couldn't believe that Jerry could be so hard and ridiculous after shooting Butch, but Cecil, whom I had married — twice — didn't lie to me, and he's the one that Jerry said it to.

Butch, furious over getting shot and then fired because he couldn't play the bass instantly for the man who shot him, sued Jerry Lee. A jury awarded him $120,000. Jerry Lee, in a similar fashion, responded to the verdict by saying, "Can you believe they gave that bastard a hundred thousand dollars?" It was definitely time to consider getting off drugs. We were both out of control.

Now, this wasn't the first or last time that many people thought Jerry Lee had harmed someone intentionally and gotten away with it. My thought, and I feel I know him better than anyone alive, is that Jerry Lee, sober and straight, would never hurt anyone. He's actually a very decent, compassionate person who has very deep-seated religious beliefs, thanks to our mother.

He has spent many, many days and nights so stoned out of his mind that I don't think he had a clue what he did, and during those periods is when most of these incidents have occurred. That's not to suggest that he's not responsible for his actions when he's like that. If he was stoned and ran over one of my kids, I'd personally kill him or anybody else that did it, damn the reason. I'm just saying that's what has caused these violent incidents, not any intention of hurting anyone that he might have had. It's just not in him.

You'll hear an awful lot said about not mixing drinking and driving. I agree with that, but Jerry Lee has convinced me that I feel even stronger about mixing drugs and guns. After one long stretch of Jerry's drug-induced insanity and tottering on the edge of perpetual overdose, cousin Jimmy Swaggart came up to Memphis and put Jerry Lee in his car and drove him to a rehab clinic in Louisiana. Jerry respected Jimmy an awful lot and never questioned his sincerity in wanting to help him. Besides, he was too doped up to argue.

After a few days at the clinic, Jerry Lee was climbing the walls. I went to visit him and found him sobered up and needing a hit in the worst way. He was none too pleased about "coming clean" at that moment. He was ranting and raving. A nurse came in, and he started demanding that she run him an IV of pure Demerol. He called it a "Demerol Drip." I'm sure that poor woman had enough of him in short order. His cute little turn of words went like, "What'ya mean NO? It's a fucking medicine, ain't it? Now go get me some Demerol and fill this here damn thing . . . you hear me? Damn it!"

Well, he seemed like he might have gone through the worst of it. Jimmy came and prayed with him and for him, and when Jimmy was with him, he would calm down and appear to be reasonable. Like all the times before, however, it didn't last long. Someone, for God knows what self-serving reason — and I have considerable suspicions of who — took it upon themselves to get Jerry what he craved.

I came in to visit him and he was flying off the ceiling. He greeted me like his long-lost buddy. "Linda Gail, I'm getting the fuck out of here." He pulled the IVs out of his arm, and still robed in his hospital gown, he reached in a bag and produced the last thing on Earth he should have had or even have been thinking about — another damn pistol! He started waving it all over the place. I could only assume it was fully loaded . . . they always were before. He started out the door, wearing his gown with his gun openly displayed in his hand.

"I promise you there ain't nobody gonna stop me, Linda Gail. Let's just be going now." He started down the hall and into the elevator. There was one poor old man in the elevator, and when he saw that Jerry Lee Lewis was hitching a ride with him, waving a pistol and talking garbage very loudly, he almost shit. Jerry Lee was, of course, social to him.

"Say there, young man, my sister and me are busting out

of this place. You want to come with us?"

"I'm sorry, Mister Lewis, sir . . . but . . . my wife is waiting for me on the third floor. It's not that I wouldn't want to go with you and I hope you don't think I'm insulting you, but my wife would be real worried if I didn't show up. You understand?"

"Absolutely, you just get right on out on the third floor. We'll be just fine." And so, he did. The sweat was pouring from his bald head as he departed.

And so, here I was, in this hospital elevator with my brother, the mad man, stoned out of his mind, waving a gun and cussing everything he saw. I truly thought, for just a moment, that nothing could be any worse. I was wrong . . . real damn wrong. I don't know whether baldy pulled the switch or what, but the fire alarms went off everywhere at the same time. And, of course, everybody in the entire hospital gathered in the main lobby of the first floor. We had almost a full house already at a standing ovation when the elevator door opened and there we stood, in all our glory.

Needless to say, panic ruled. The lobby emptied quicker than if flames had been bursting out of the elevator instead of us. Jerry was screaming at everyone, threatening to kill anybody who tried to stop him, not that anyone was. We went straight to the parking lot, got in the car and drove to a liquor store where Jerry Lee got a bottle of Jack Daniels. He finished it off by himself and passed out in the back seat of the car. He didn't go back to the hospital. His drying out periods never worked.

On another occasion, while he was sober, we were on the Jet Commander on the way to a show. I was sitting beside Jerry Lee when he pulled out a pistol. He was waving it around and scaring me to death. He knew he was torturing me and found it great sport. "Linda Gail," he said, "if this gun went off, if I put one little hole through the pressurized walls of this plane . . . you know what you'd get?"

"What's that?"

"You'd get the greatest blow job of the century. You, me and everything in this entire plane would get sucked out of the bullet hole. Did you know that?"

All I knew is that I wanted him to put it away and never touch another one. He was playing with fire every time he picked up one of those cursed things. I must have been the only Lewis offspring not fascinated with guns. Even Frankie Jean carries one with her all the time. This began very early on with her also.

Jerry Lee has a long-time friend named Dagwood, and Dagwood has a reputation as a dangerous man — a gangster, if you will. He was the friend who gave Jerry Lee the .357 Magnum pistol he punctuated Butch Owens chest with. Jerry Lee and the band were doing a benefit show in Ferriday. Frankie Jean was driving them back to the airport after the show in her Suburban, a cross between a Ford Explorer and a dump-truck. An argument began and amidst all the screaming, Frankie Jean pulled over the car and got out her pistol. She was hot. Jerry Lee knew not to cross her. The minute the wheels quit turning on the vehicle, Jerry Lee and the entire band started running from her line of sight.

Now, Dagwood was not a man to be easily frightened. He walked up to Frankie Jean and brazenly asked, "Why don't you just put that gun away? You know you're not going to shoot anybody."

Let's pick this story up several years later. Dagwood was at Jerry Lee's house in Memphis. Jerry Lee remarked casually to him that his sister was bringing her kids over to swim in the pool. I was there and thought it odd that this seemed to upset Dagwood. He said something to the effect of, "I'm getting out of here." He wasn't kidding. He disappeared until after Frankie Jean and her kids had left.

When I saw him again, I asked him what the problem was. He explained that previously, when he had approached Frankie and asked her just who she thought she was going to shoot, she put the barrel of the pistol directly between his eyes and cocked the hammer. He continued, "Linda Gail, I've known a lot of men that have shot other people over the years; I've even had occasion to do it myself. I know what it takes to pull the trigger. I can see in a person's eyes if they are going to actually do it. When I asked your sister who she was going to shoot, she put her finger on the trigger, her hands didn't shake at all, and I could feel that she was really going to kill me. My whole life flashed before me and then, she just let it pass. She's completely capable of pulling the trigger. I'm not going to cross that woman." He had learned what we had always known.

I probably shouldn't mention this, but early in her last marriage, Frankie got into an argument with her husband, and she actually stabbed him. His ass went to the hospital to get stitched up. He must have had it coming, because he's still with her, many years later.

Even though I wasn't shooting or stabbing anybody, I was not in much better shape than Jerry Lee. Our lives had consisted mainly of a few great hours a week on stage, doing the one thing we did right and feeling the satisfaction. And that sensation was stronger than the pull of sanity.

Chapter Nine:
Of Love *and*
Many
Marriages

Our personal lives were a wreck. We had both put a number of marriages on the rocks. I not only had gone through the marriage to Bobby Goza at fourteen, but also to a neighbor, Jim Bushland. Jim was in the Navy, and we got married on a furlough weekend. After four days of the best screwing ever, he returned to the sea and that was the end of that.

In 1963, I married the most unlikely of suitors, Jerry Lee's best friend, Cecil Harrelson. He was more like a brother than a romantic interest. I guess I felt comfortable with him, and I did know him pretty well. We were around each other a lot. One night, we were at a party at the Manhattan Club in Memphis, listening to a great black entertainer named Willie Mitchell. We had too much to drink and wound up in a motel room. I got pregnant with Cecil Jr. I didn't consider an abortion, as my upbringing would never have allowed that. I trusted Cecil and we both wanted the best for this child, so we got married.

Cecil was and is a good man. Even though I loved Cecil and respected him, our love life suffered because I never felt quite right in bed with him. It was like I was with a relative. My God, he was there with my brother when I was born. As much as we wanted this marriage to work, it just wasn't meant to be. By 1965, I was having an affair with an attorney who was absolutely gorgeous, and that union ended.

In 1969, I married Kenny Lovelace, a long-time band member and close friend of Jerry Lee's who still travels with him. It was kind of bizarre traveling with a man who I had been married to (Cecil) and another man that I was now married to. To top it off, they were all friends. I guess the only way it could have gotten any weirder was for me to divorce Kenny and remarry Cecil. It didn't happen all that quickly and simply, but yes, it did happen. I told you — we're different.

As great a guy as Kenny was when he was sober and while we were single, after we married he'd get drunk and abusive. I might be a lot of things, but someone who would lay back and tolerate that, I'm not. We were quickly apart. As soon as we separated, we became friends again, and that's how we've remained to this day.

Next, came an affair with Judd Phillips, Jr., called Juddy by his friends. He was Judd Phillips' son, and no, I never told him that I had a short affair with his father. I guess he will know now. If we were married, I'd be divorcing again, I suppose. We had a beautiful daughter, Mary Jean. If anybody ever had rock 'n' roll genes, it should be her. Her uncles include Jerry Lee Lewis and Sam Phillips. Juddy couldn't marry me, so good old Cecil did it again. That way, Mary Jean would have a daddy. And, once again, we divorced a year later.

I have to laugh at some of these interludes when I look back. Most of the time, I didn't even worry about getting a divorce. When I had enough, I'd just leave. Or, if I got an offer I liked better, that was sufficient reason to make a change. I'd get ready to marry the next one, and invariably the attorney would tell me that I was still married to one of the others. He'd take care of it, and I would become the next Mrs. Whoever it was I married. There were some better ones to come, but let's talk a little about how Jerry Lee was doing in the area of romance.

Jerry Lee would, because of circumstances, marry only six times in contrast to my eight husbands. This shortcoming on his part can probably be attributed to the difficulty of trying to marry someone whose name you don't know — which is who Jerry Lee spent most of his nights with, even when he had a wife at home. He had married Dorothy, Jane and Myra in fairly short order. The marriage to Myra lasted for thirteen years, though he and she set no records for their contributions to the institution or fidelity. During the declining years of that marriage, Jerry Lee pushed the art of cocktail waitress courting to new highs in the industry. I overheard someone say of his ego, "It's not surprising to me that he's got such a big head. As many blow jobs as he's had, I'm surprised his head isn't just one big bubble." That's not as far off as that observer might have thought.

There was a real funny occurrence that was brought on by all of Jerry Lee's affairs with less than desirable mates and his decidedly less than desirable financial responsibility.

Jerry Lee had found the home in Memphis that he decreed would be his castle for life. It is to this day. It's a beautiful place, with all the luxuries that you would expect. It's got to be worth millions.

Jerry Lee was aware of his less-than-stable ways, so he took the full asking price of the house, about $120,000 in those days, and gave it to Cecil. "Now Cecil," he said, "I want you to buy this place for me and fix it in such a way that nobody can ever take it from me — not a wife, a woman, the IRS, the law . . . nobody. Can you do that?" Cecil knew exactly what had to be done and did it. He took the money and bought it in his own name, which is how it remains to this day. Jerry Lee has life-long rights to occupy it and then, guess who it belongs to. That's right, Cecil.

Now, as bad a deal as that may seem, it has proven to be a good move on more than one occasion. I can remember one particularly beautiful spring day, I was up at the house with Cecil when Jerry Lee came driving up in his Rolls Royce convertible with his new flame. This was a beautiful creature, known particularly by band members for her unique pneumatic capabilities, which certainly would make her a hit with Jerry Lee who apparently was always a little low on air pressure. This young woman, and she was incredibly beautiful, remained Jerry Lee's mistress for a number of years. Her name was Charlotte but Jerry Lee called her "Pumpkin." Anyway, this spring day, they pulled up and Jerry Lee called out to Cecil, who went over with me close behind. Jerry was feeling no pain and apparently in a generous mood. He started in on Cecil.

"Now, Cecil, I want you go draw up the papers and give this place here to Pumpkin. She's a fine thing, and she just loves this place." I'm sure she did. Needless to say, Cecil had heard it many times before. I think this one was the last straw for Cecil. He turned to me when Jerry Lee and Pumpkin drove off and said, "Linda Gail, I'm done with Jerry Lee. I've had enough. I'm going home to Sandy Bayou, and I won't be back." That's exactly what he did. He nonetheless kept the house in his name.

On a much more recent occasion, Jerry Lee's present wife, Kerrie called up Cecil and made her best pitch.

"Cecil, Jerry Lee and I have gotten all our financial problems behind us and even have the IRS happy. We'd like for you to draw up the papers and put our home back in our names."

Cecil responded predictably. "I'll tell you just what I told all those other whores that called me up. Nope, not now, not never!" And he hung up the phone. Now that's a man that can keep a promise. It doesn't hurt, I suppose, that it will probably put millions in his wallet one day.

After Myra, Jerry Lee married Jaren — an ill-fated marriage that ended after they had been separated and at odds for quite some time. She took an overdose and drowned in the pool.

It wasn't long after this that the Internal Revenue Service descended on Jerry. I think to this day that Jaren's death was the real cause for those problems. Jerry Lee does have a temper, and I have seen him do some things when he was high that disgusted even me. I know a lot of people bought into the murder theory, but I just don't believe it for a minute. He would not murder anyone.

An accident? Possibly, but he would have to have been blitzed out of his mind. If he was, then it would have been an accident, not murder. I'm sure that if the police had thought he killed Jaren, they would have at least filed charges against him. They certainly didn't mind doing that on several occasions for a number of lesser offenses.

Cecil Harrelson had always taken care of Jerry Lee's financial affairs. He eventually grew tired of dealing with Jerry Lee and left the road life permanently, even though he still remains friends with all of us. He was a good manager and kept Jerry Lee's finances in top shape. He made sure that receipts were kept when the band was on the road, and when taxes were due, he'd call up Jerry Lee and say, "Jerry Lee, you owe ten thousand" or whatever the amount was. Jerry Lee would go off his rocker for a while saying his usual, "Fuck the bastards . . . not another damn cent," etc., etc. Cecil would listen till Jerry Lee started running out of wind and then say something to the order of, "Jerry Lee, you owe it, you made the money, you've got to pay it." Jerry Lee would rant a little more and then give in 'cause he knew Cecil was right. "Go ahead, write the damn check." And he would.

After Cecil quit, a "professional" manager took over. When taxes were due, he would go through the same scenario with Jerry Lee except, when Jerry Lee said, "Fuck them! Not another cent," he was intimidated and did just that. He didn't send in the money and before long, the IRS came knocking. They placed a lien on Jerry Lee's earnings and searched the house, selling everything of value they could prove belonged to Jerry Lee.

One thing they confiscated of special interest was a tape of master recordings that Jerry Lee had made but never released. They sold it to the highest bidder, who turned out to be the Bear Family record company in Europe, who released it internationally. It even has an impromptu sermon on it where Jerry Lee was going through a quasi-evangelical period and was preaching to everyone in the studio. They left it live on the album, and it's right interesting to listen to. The record has become a very high-priced collector's piece, selling for about $400 in good shape. Thank God the house was in Cecil's name. Otherwise, it would have been given up for taxes, pussy or both.

Jerry Lee's sixth wife was a cocktail waitress from Michigan named Shawn. Of all Jerry Lee's wives and lovers, this was the one great love of his life. She was, like many others, a very beautiful young woman. The marriage was stormy. Anybody who had to put up with Jerry Lee's bizarre lifestyle and spoiled behavior would have had problems getting along with him. But she was special to Jerry Lee.

I visited with her at Jerry Lee's house in Memphis, and it was apparent that she was heavily into drugs. She was sitting on a couch across from me talking, with very slurred speech, and I asked if she was all right. Of course, she said she was, but while she was talking, a bottle of pills fell out of her purse and onto the floor. She was having drugs supplied to her by Dr. Nick once again. She said she was just having trouble sleeping. I wouldn't see her alive again. One week later, she died of an overdose.

This did not go unnoticed by a number of the media who saw a murder and conspiracy in the making. *Rolling Stone* magazine did a real hatchet job on Jerry Lee that outright accused him of murdering her. Jerry Lee wasn't even there when she drowned. Her sister Karen was married to an FBI agent, and they were either suspicious that Jerry Lee was involved or were just disgusted with him for the lifestyle that came with being married to him.

As much as they had been arguing, Shawn's death still tore Jerry Lee up like no other woman ever had. He sang "Only You" at her funeral and cried like a baby. He buried her in Ferriday. Jerry Lee's detractors said he'd murdered another wife. "Bullshit," is the best reply I can make to that. He loved her and wouldn't have lifted a finger against her.

Shawn's sister could best be described as aspiring to become poor white trash. She would come to parties and family gatherings at Jerry Lee's with tight, cut away shorts that exposed half of the cheeks of her butt. She wore a tube top with no bra and kept a cigarette hanging out of her mouth. The chief point of conversation that she constantly pursued with Shawn and Jerry Lee was her need for Jerry Lee's money. After Shawn died, Geraldo Rivera had her sister on his show, all cleaned up like a Sunday School teacher accusing Jerry Lee of murdering her loving sister. It was cheap-shot journalism put forward with a bias — a twisted truth to attract TV viewers and nothing else.

Jerry Lee endured a series of tragic losses: two wives, his mother and father, and his son Steve Allen, by Myra. But the death that changed him most was that of his son, Jerry Lee Lewis, Jr., by his second wife Jane. He was killed at the age of eighteen in a freak accident while he was towing a Jeep with another car.

He had been going through some problem years, like any kid at home without his father. He was living in Louisiana with his mother and was more than she could handle. So Jane sent him to live with Jerry Lee in Memphis. He had been coming along great, and his daddy and he had gotten real close. Jerry Lee was always helping him with old cars, getting him motorcycles and a lot of things that boys that age love. He was also spending time with him and even letting him go on the road with the band. His death absolutely broke Jerry Lee's heart.

When he was buried in Ferriday, Jerry Lee took his girlfriend Charlotte to the funeral. She and his then-wife Jaren got into an argument about who was going to sit up front with Jerry Lee. With everybody in the place listening, Jerry Lee turned to them both and told them loudly that he didn't care who sat where, as long as he could sit where he could see Junior. It was gut wrenching for everybody there.

With all of the torment these highly unusual and horrible events brought to Jerry Lee's life, he turned, for a brief period, back to his roots — the church. There was a preacher, the Reverend C. M. Newton of the Church of God in Memphis, who liked Jerry Lee and let him start preaching there on Sundays. Now, for all his craziness and wild antics, Jerry Lee does know the Bible. His mother and the Holiness Church in Ferriday were still right there inside him. He knew scripture and Bible verses as good as any preacher.

It seems only obvious that anybody who thought enough of all those rules in the Bible to memorize them, would have a lot of conflict inside if they chose not to follow the teachings. This war is still going on inside Jerry Lee. It's a classical battle between God, who gives Jerry the talent, the soul and the music, and the Devil, who wants to use these very same talents to bring him down and everybody he loves with him.

Chapter Ten:
Even
Evangelists
Get Horny

Jerry Lee was not the only family member having problems. Poor old cousin Jimmy was up to his neck in them. His ministry had been one of the great pioneering efforts in televangelism. He had become as well known throughout the world as Jerry Lee. He was even known in a lot of the remote countries where Jerry Lee was not as well known as he was. And, let's tell it like it is — he was making a great deal of money.

Now, I don't have any problem with that. I think that the best in any profession should be financially rewarded for being good at what they do. Why should preachers be left out of the loop? They have to eat, buy cars, send their kids to college and pay for a place to live, just like everybody else. Jimmy was at the top of his industry and doing a lot of good in the process.

I could picture Momma, her sisters and the little church in Ferriday every time I heard him preach. Just like Jerry Lee, it was all there, just inside of him. I guess the only difference between them is that Jimmy's upbringing, with the abuse of Uncle Son, had put a lot more of the fear of the Devil in him than Jerry Lee had inside. Seeing what was happening to Jerry Lee had to reinforce those beliefs considerably, not that they weren't strong enough already.

Listen to Jimmy when he plays the piano, and you can literally hear the Jerry Lee Lewis style of piano playing there, just as you can with Mickey Gilley. Jimmy could have been very successful just as a musician if he had wanted to. Mickey proved that there was room in the family for more than one star. Another would have been no problem.

All three cousins were at their peak at the same time. Mickey was the driving force behind the Urban Cowboy movement that fostered an entire new sound of country music, several movies, lots of new stars and a hoard of new fans that never had any interest in country music prior to then. He was getting filthy rich, too. And he was the best of the three at hanging on to it. He invested wisely and today is a very, very rich man. Jerry Lee was backsliding and poor old Jimmy was about to suffer ridicule beyond all reason for what was actually pretty insignificant compared to all the good he had done.

Jimmy's wife, Frances, was a good woman, although she was pretty damned stiff. I just have to believe that maybe there wasn't much to their love life. As I have mentioned numerous times before, to be a Lewis is to suffer from a good measure of being oversexed. Those two facts being mixed together could cause even a casual observer to gather that Jimmy might feel just a little lust in his heart, to borrow a Presidential expression from another Jimmy.

Now, Jim Bakker is a tiny little man. He was, I guess you would say, a competitor of cousin Jimmy's. He was up in Charlotte, North Carolina, getting rich off something called the PTL Club. They were selling Christians time shares in a multi-million-dollar resort that would have looked perfect on the strip in Vegas. Jim Bakker and his lovely, though a little overpainted wife, Tammy Faye, drew a huge television audience that had to drain a little, or probably a lot, of the money from cousin Jimmy's operation. It seems that a lot of people became more than a little unhappy when they discovered that the time-share condo they had been promised for a fixed number of days a year had been sold to so many God-fearing souls that they would be lucky to see that room for one day out of every five years. Now, I've heard an expression for years that goes, "Slow to anger, quick to forgive." Apparently, Jim Bakker's group of followers thought that was an inappropriate response to having their pockets picked, and they took his butt to court.

Sensing a little weakness in his competitor, cousin Jimmy went for the jugular, so to speak. Week after week, Sunday after Sunday, he would rake Jim and Tammy Faye over the Holy coals of Hellfire on national television. When his own business started picking back up as a result, he became perhaps a little overaggressive.

Personally, I could take it all but the crying. Jimmy does the best cry on cue that I've ever seen. It's just a little too much for my particular taste. Once in a while, maybe at a funeral or a sad movie, but not every time I turn on the TV. I think that was his undoing. To be believed when you cry so much, people have to see you as some sort of religious fanatic, which, of course, is really funny in this particular case, since Jimmy is.

And what about Jessica Hahn, the church secretary who claimed that Jim Bakker took advantage of her? She was such a devout woman that I swear I could almost see a halo around her in the five-page, full nude layout that *Penthouse* magazine did of her. Holy Nipples, Batman! Her boobs were bigger than Jim Bakker, and she wants us to believe that he took advantage of her? If there is any justice in the next life, she'll be doin' time as a hunchback leper.

Jim Bakker finally got sent to the Big House for a long, long rest. Don't you know, as sissy looking as he always was, that going to prison made him feel like a female French poodle being put in a pen with a thousand hunting hounds that hadn't even smelled one in five years? My butt puckers just thinking about it. And Tammy Faye, she bailed out of the whole affair with Jim's best friend, who had gotten the lion's share of the money Jim stole by building the PTL Resort. Ain't it always the same? And they call us the weaker sex. It just never made sense to me.

Apparently, cousin Jimmy was the big winner. All those millions of viewers had to find a new preacher to send their money to every week, and he, as the staunchest critic of Jim Bakker, stood to collect from most of them, especially the disenchanted. I guess all that winning made his mind turn to a little bit of recreation.

So, cousin Jimmy finally got horny and decided to pay a woman of the night to undress for him. All I can say is, What's so horrible about that? I am more concerned about the people in society who want to pay our police to run around chasing after somebody who wants to watch somebody take their clothes off (willingly, I might add). I personally would prefer they spend *all* of their time and talents tracking down murderers, rapists, terrorists and things of that nature. I doubt that very few people who are getting laid enough are out blowing up shopping malls or shooting planes out of the sky.

Well, the young woman helped the police make an example of cousin Jimmy. Here they had caught this high profile evangelist out watching somebody naked. I just can't believe it to this day. Poor Jimmy had to be mortified. And Aunt Frances, I'm sure that Jimmy would rather have served Jim Bakker's sentence than have her find out what he had been up to. To me, after spending forty-nine years with Jerry Lee, Jimmy Swaggart is as close to a living saint as I have ever personally known.

As sad as that little affair was, it didn't end there. It ended a short time later with an even more pathetic episode. This one is so sad it's funny. Jimmy was out in California, a pretty long way from home. He apparently needed to take another peek. He was cruising the local red light district in his Lincoln Town Car. I guess he was more than just a little nervous after the last venture outside of his congregation.

In his car were a number of what you could call "skin books." I'm actually very happy about men liking to look at women's bodies and even wanting to do a lot more than look. It is, after all, what has kept the human race going since the Garden of Eden. At least they were skin books with women in them, so he was in the mainstream in that regard.

Well, picture cousin Jimmy, driving down this rather dirty side of town, his last attempt at this very thing causing him to be arrested and practically ruining everything he had done over a thirty-year period. I'm sure he was more than a little nervous. About that time, a black and white squad car made a U-turn behind him. He had seen them approach and knew for sure that they must be after him. Now remember, he had done absolutely nothing wrong at this point. His nerves overcame him and he could just see himself being arrested again (for what? possession of dirty books?). He did what any rational person would have done at a moment like that — he started pitching the skin books out the car window. The policeman, who was incidentally paying no attention to Jimmy prior to then, pulled him over to find out what he had been throwing out of his car. This next arrest served to finish off whatever credibility Jimmy had left as a preacher, or least that's what everyone thought then.

You see, preaching is a lot like any other type of entertaining. Just like Jerry Lee had become more of a legendary figure by fighting back and surviving in the face of very bad odds, so has cousin Jimmy. He kept preaching wherever he could. He begged for forgiveness and owned up to his wanton ways in front of two or ten thousand, and he cried far better than ever before. Next Sunday morning, cut on you TV and channel surf for a while. If you don't find a national channel with cousin Jimmy on it begging for your money, I'll kiss your rosy red.

What did Jerry Lee think about Jimmy's problems? He went to see Mickey Gilley perform in Las Vegas sometime after Jimmy had all his problems. It was a large club with a big audience; everyone was oblivious to the fact that Jerry Lee was in the crowd. Cousin Mickey made the mistake of telling a joke about Jimmy's problems. Jerry Lee stood up in the audience, right in the middle of Mickey's act, and cussed him out. "How dare you make fun of God's chosen! You'll go to hell for doing that. How dare you!" Needless to say, there were a lot of stunned faces in the audience. I'm sure that if Jerry Lee had been doing a show there at the time, they would have told him, "You'll never work in Vegas again."

Chapter Eleven:
Dick Clark Ages

There's a famous book and later a movie called *The Portrait of Dorian Gray*. It's about a guy who makes a pact with the Devil to stay young forever. Instead of him aging, a portrait of him ages. He wines and dines and squires the young women while this oil painting begins to look like a dried up prune. I always thought that this novel was based on the life of Dick Clark. I swear, he must have such a painting hidden in a closet somewhere. He hasn't aged a day in the last forty years. He's got to be at least a hundred or so.

As I mentioned earlier, Dick Clark was one of the first to abandon Jerry Lee when he married cousin Myra. I always find it particularly disgusting when show business personalities start judging other people's morals. My God, if it hasn't been done in Hollywood, it hasn't been done. That said, I'm sure that Dick Clark is not Philadelphia's answer to John the Baptist. Nonetheless, Dick decided that Jerry Lee was not morally fit to entertain the youth of America, so he boycotted his records religiously.

Many years passed. Jerry Lee was in his second or third rebirth as an entertainer. Dick Clark was producing a TV rock 'n' roll show, and he desperately wanted Jerry Lee to be on it. Elvis was dead (I guess he didn't have a portrait). If you wanted to stage a tribute to the birth of rock 'n' roll and you couldn't get Elvis, who else comes to mind that personifies that short period of time when Sun Records ruled the airways? That's right, Jerry Lee is the only other centerpiece for the time.

Dick Clark called Jerry Lee as if nothing had ever happened. A very interesting conversation took place, as you might expect.

"Jerry Lee . . . how are you? Good, great! This is Dick Clark. I was wondering if maybe you might like to headline a major TV show I'm putting together, old friend. What do you say?"

To his credit and upbringing, Jerry Lee did not immediately say, "Kiss my ass, you two-faced son of a bitch. I haven't forgotten for a minute how you treated me." Nope, instead Jerry Lee invited him to come visit in Memphis for a few days — you know, old times, a get-to-know-each-other-again time. Dick agreed.

Dick showed up shortly thereafter at Jerry Lee's house in Memphis. He tactfully avoided talking about the show right off the bat and instead let Jerry Lee pick the topics to talk about and places to visit. He was waiting for just the right moment to smooth talk old Jerry Lee into doing the show.

The times had changed. Marrying your thirteen-year-old cousin looked fairly tame compared to modern events, like murdering your folks as they slept or having group sex with only one sex present.

Jerry Lee kept Dick Clark going day and night for four days. He insisted that Dick hang with the "real" Jerry Lee for a while. Anyway, on the fourth day of this love-fest, Jerry Lee suggested that Dick, Jerry Lee and I go out to the Nightlighter, probably the most famous nightspot ever in Memphis. Many's the night there that an unsuspecting audience got a free four-hour concert from Jerry Lee while he blew it out. He would get high and perform for whoever was there. It happened so often for a while that patrons came expecting to see Jerry Lee. I have soloed there many times also, and it is a great club for the sort of intimacy with a responsive audience that musicians love.

Jerry Lee dragged poor old Dick Clark down there about nine in the evening. The crowd went berserk when they saw Jerry Lee walk in, and in short order he was at the piano, entertaining the troops. After the third hour of what was really a great performance, Jerry Lee came back to the table, looked at Dick and said, "I've made my decision about your show, Dick."

Dick's eyes lighted up as if he just knew his four-day investment had paid off. "That's great, Jerry Lee. You'll do it then, the show?"

Jerry Lee smiled and looked him dead in the eyes. "Nope, I've decided I ain't doing it. Thanks for asking though."

With that, Jerry Lee returned to the piano, and a dejected Dick sat back down beside me, looking fairly exhausted. He turned to me and said with great conviction, "Linda Gail, your brother is one cross I cannot bear." I thought to myself, What a great line. All I can say is, Dick Clark severely underestimated Jerry Lee's memory if he thought a few days of kissing his ass would make him come around just to be on television.

It was during this major rebirth of Jerry Lee's career that a unique thing happened. I have never heard of anything close to this happening to another entertainer. Jerry Lee was booked to perform for a live, sold-out crowd in Paris, France. He had been driving and abusing himself for a good while, and on the day of the concert just said, "The hell with it. I ain't goin'." He didn't bother to call and inform anyone of his decision, he just forgot about it. The crowd was seated, waiting for him to appear, and two thousand miles away, Jerry Lee was asleep in his bed in Memphis.

The promoters were going nuts and saw not just a huge financial loss, but also the possibility of getting physically hurt. This crowd was getting loud and nasty. In an absolute panic, they called Memphis and got Jerry Lee on the phone. They pleaded with him to come over and said they would make arrangements to have him picked up, and he could sleep all the way over if he wanted. "Just come. Whatever you need, we'll do it!"

Reluctantly, Jerry Lee agreed. A private Lear jet was chartered and flown into Memphis to pick up Jerry Lee, who they had driven to the airport. The Lear jet transported him to New York, where he was transferred to the Concord which travels at supersonic speeds, and he was flown to Paris. Believe it or not, when he arrived almost ten hours later, the crowd was all still in place, waiting for his appearance. It was practically the middle of the night. Jerry Lee put on a fabulous show, and the crowd, who should have been ready to lynch him, loved him. They had become part of the Jerry Lee Lewis legend in one of the most bizarre no-shows ever.

Let's put another myth to bed. A lot of media types, press,

anti-Jerry Lee idiots and troublemakers in general have, for years, built up a fictitious war between Elvis and Jerry Lee. Now, I'm not going to say that there was not competitiveness between them. All performers have that in them in relation to other performers. They need to have the feeling of "I'm the best" or they couldn't get on the stage with the confidence that's necessary to be a big-time performer. It's just the same as getting in a boxing ring, or putting on a football helmet in the NFL, or knowing you're going to have to guard Michael Jordan for two halves of basketball. You have to feel you are as good or better than all the competition to get out on the floor. It was that way with Jerry Lee and Elvis.

That aside, they were good friends. They hung out together during the early years at Sun Records. They rode motorcycles and partied many times. After all, they were both still teenagers when they met, just a couple of good old country boys who had a lot in common. The friendship remained as they got older, even though their paths didn't cross all that often.

I can remember going to a party that Elvis threw at the Manhattan Club in Memphis. I got up in my skin-tight skirt and did a couple of songs with Elvis listening. What a thrill! Later, one of my friends told me that Elvis had said to them, "She's really hot!" Did that ever make my day. Any woman who was not turned on by a young Elvis Presley needs to have her estrogen level checked.

When Elvis began his first appearance in Las Vegas, on opening night he sent a plane to pick up Jerry Lee and the entire band. They were all his guests that evening, with a front-row table for the show. I don't think you would do that for someone you didn't like a lot. After the show, Elvis, his entourage, Jerry Lee and the guys in his band all got together backstage for an impromptu party. They were drinking liquor (that's right, Elvis too) and singing.

Elvis had a piano in his dressing room. Before Jerry Lee had left for Vegas, I had taught him a new song I had just written called "Love of All Seasons." He played it for Elvis and then they started doing it together. Elvis loved it and said that Jerry Lee shouldn't do that one, it was more his type of song. Jerry Lee immediately sensed that if Elvis was interested in it, it must be a winner. He told Elvis that he had promised me that he was going to record it and declined to let Elvis do it. If I had been there, I would have personally strangled him. If Elvis had recorded it, I'd still be getting the royalty checks on it today. Jerry Lee did record it on an album, and it died a simple death. Oh well, fate works in mysterious ways.

As the party continued, everyone was getting a little wasted and louder. The door opened and in walked the illustrious Colonel Tom Parker. He came over to Elvis and said, "Elvis, it's time for you to go to bed. You've got shows again tomorrow, and you need your rest. Tell these folks good night."

A wasted Kenny Lovelace walked over to the Colonel and asked him just who he thought he was. The Colonel explained that the one thing he *wasn't* was high and that Elvis would be leaving. Jerry Lee then got in the Colonel's face and started on him.

"Elvis, I wouldn't let no son of a bitch tell me what the hell I could and couldn't do. What do you think of that, Sergeant Parker?"

Unamused, the Colonel merely answered, "Elvis, let's go." Sheepishly, Elvis told everyone good night and left with the

Colonel. He was completely under his control. Little did Jerry Lee realize that not too much later in the future, his life would be controlled in a similar fashion and that it would extend even into his own home.

They remained friends right up till Elvis died. A lot has been made of the "Eldorado Incident" at the gates to Graceland. This is what really happened, according to Jerry Lee, who I have never caught telling me a lie. He says that Elvis, who was already in his declining years, was very depressed. He felt like he was a prisoner at Graceland, which, when you look at the facts, he was. My God, people *camped out* by his gates for days just to get a quick peek at him sitting in the back of his limousine. He couldn't even go out with bodyguards; he was literally a bird in a guilded cage. How would you feel if the only way you could go see a movie was if you rented the entire theater? This couldn't occur until after all of the "regular" folks who had paid their two bucks (back then) had seen the show and gone parking with their dates.

So, Elvis called Jerry Lee and said something to the effect that he needed to "get out" for awhile. Now, he might have meant to just get away without an entourage for a few hours. Or, he might have just wanted to spend a little time with Jerry Lee remembering what things were like when they started out together so many years earlier. But Jerry Lee was, as usual during that time period, stoned out of his gourd. He thought that when Elvis said "get out," he meant, "Come break me out of here!"

Jerry Lee got in his new Cadillac Eldorado and headed for Graceland. When he got to the gate, the guard recognized who it was and went to ask what he wanted. Jerry Lee said he told the guard that he had come to "break Elvis out of here." It was about then that the guard noticed the gun laying on the front seat beside Jerry Lee. It was a large-caliber pistol, just like the one he carried with him practically every waking minute. The astute sentry asked Jerry Lee what he was going to do with the gun, and Jerry Lee smart-mouthed him by answering, "Why, shoot Elvis, of course."

The guard went back to the shack and called the police. Jerry Lee grew impatient waiting and revved up the Caddy. A few more minutes went by and Jerry Lee got more and more agitated with the lack of response to his request to see Elvis. It was then that he decided to crash the gates with his car, which he did. The gates were more than substantial and the car took a whale of a hit.

About the time that Jerry Lee tried to get out of the car, a contingent of Memphis' finest men in blue had him surrounded and placed him under arrest. The biggest thing he was guilty of was being high and incoherent, and just wanting to help his friend. Not only was Elvis not concerned about Jerry Lee harming him in any way, he immediately bailed Jerry Lee out of jail. Just a few weeks later, Elvis was dead.

#

Jerry Lee has his opinion of where he should rank in the history books regarding music in this century. Everyone will not like him and that doesn't bother him at all. He has accomplished what he started out to do, and he deservedly commands a certain amount of recognition for that. As a matter of fact, he demands it. He was, after all, the first person inducted into the Rock 'n' Roll hall of fame.

Bernard Porter has handled a lot of appearances for Jerry Lee. He called Memphis very excited recently with a strong offer. Kerrie, wife number seven, answered his call.

"Kerrie, the 'David Letterman Show' called. David wants to know if Jerry Lee will sit in with Paul Shaffer and the band on their show. Only a few great instrumentalists are ever asked to do it. It's a huge honor; only the likes of B.B. King and monster acts get asked. What do you say?"

"Forget it Bernard, Jerry Lee would never appear in somebody's band just playing like a sideman," said Kerrie.

"But . . . the Letterman show is the biggest show in the world. It's like having a hit record. I know Jerry would want to do it."

They bantered back and forth with Bernard telling her why Jerry Lee should do the show and Kerrie saying he wouldn't even consider it. Kerrie eventually got tired of arguing with Bernard and transferred the call to Jerry Lee's bedroom, where he was resting. She called to him over the phone.

"Jerry Lee, Bernard says the Letterman show wants you to sit in and do a number with the band."

All that could be heard from Jerry Lee was several loud outbursts of laughter and then the clicking of the receiver as he hung up the phone. He doesn't do sit-ins with anybody.

Chapter Twelve: It's Time to Try Normal

Mother's death just about destroyed the entire family. She was our foundation, the emotional rock that we all counted on for stability. After Daddy left us, Momma was still there, all the time.

I remember once, when Jerry Lee was a very big star with number-one records, she was backstage as he was being interviewed by a mob of reporters. One of them asked a question about his mother being there with him, and he gave a smartass answer that Momma took offense at. She got right in his face with everyone watching and said, "Do you know who you're talking to? You are talking to your mother, boy, and I'll slap you down. You better not forget it!"

Jerry Lee looked over at me and shrugged. He turned to Momma in front of the group and said merely, "Yes, Momma."

She was always very supportive of all her children. She

never remarried after Daddy left, and I feel it was because of us. For one thing, I think she reasoned that if she remarried, Jerry Lee might not feel as compelled to help us as he did, and that I might suffer in return. I was spoiled beyond belief back then by Momma's two housekeepers. I didn't even pick up my dirty panties. I was completely rotten. God, those were the days.

Momma always stayed strong in her Holiness religious beliefs, right up to her death. Now, she always fit in with whatever group she was with, and she was not above taking a drink in the right setting, though never to get even high. And, in disregard to her religious background, she wore makeup and beautiful designer clothes. Momma even had a clothes designer in California, Mr. Sydney. But possessions never impressed her, and she always remained the same. When she died, it sent us into a tailspin.

Jerry Lee and the entire band were getting a reputation as a drug problem band. One groupie-type fan called the DEA (Drug Enforcement Agency) and said that they knew for a fact the band was not only carrying around a shitload of drugs with them, but that they also had a small baby they had kidnapped, and they were giving the baby drugs! Well, the baby was certainly not kidnapped — it was Lee, Jerry Lee's son by Kerrie. Jerry Lee would take his own life before he would allow anything to happen to Lee. In many respects, Lee *is* Jerry Lee's life.

Nevertheless, with the horrible reputation we had, the DEA was there to greet us as we arrived at the airport. Unbelievably, they stopped Jerry Lee, Kerrie and me and checked our bags for drugs, which, of course, we did not have. Any drugs either of us would have been taking would have been prescription drugs anyway. The remarkable part of this affair was that our band was allowed to take all of their luggage and head to the hotel while they questioned and searched us. Had they taken the time and thought to check the band, we would have been playing with no accompaniment for a long time.

I began taking Quaaludes by the handfuls and became heavily addicted. I had figured out by then that the way to acquire legal prescription drugs in mega-quantities was to visit from three to five doctors and give them the symptoms, which I knew only too well would result in a legal prescription for Quaaludes. Now, nobody ever wakes up one day and says to themself, "I think that I'm going to become addicted to drugs today. I think I'll destroy my entire life." No, you start with a pill at night to help you sleep. Then two, then five, then a handful several times a day. It happens over an extended period of time and in a very insidious way. You're hooked before you understand that you have a problem.

I overdosed to the point of nearly killing myself four or five times. The last time I overdosed, in 1974, I was hospitalized for quite a while and came to the realization that I could not continue on the road without winding up in an early grave. They had taken me to the mental ward at Baptist Hospital in Memphis. If I had to give a one-word description of what it's like to wind up in that situation, the word would be "degrading."

I would scream and curse the nurses for not giving me the drugs my body was craving. When you are that close to dying from overdosing, you lose control of your bodily functions. So, these very women, these magnificent human beings who understood and never lashed back at the spoiled little bitch who had everything most people wanted and pissed it all away, would clean the urine and shit off of my body and tuck me in bed. God bless them!

I feel obligated to also mention that I did not have a lick of medical insurance. Jerry Lee provided medical coverage for every member of the band, but, like a lot of policies, it didn't cover self-inflicted overdoses or mental problems. Jerry Lee paid the entire bill for me. It was over $20,000. That was a great deal of money for him to come up with, but he has never even mentioned it to me, no matter how bad his finances became.

Jerry Lee was also real strung out on drugs, and after I had come so close to losing it all, I wanted no more part of the drug culture. Jerry was becoming verbally abusive of me, and I had about as much of all of that scene as I could stand.

During one show, I missed a cue to start singing backup, and even though no one in the audience would have been aware that I hadn't come in when I should have, Jerry Lee stopped playing and asked over the microphone, in front of the whole crowd, if I had any idea of what the hell I was doing. He then said that we would try it one more time. We all started the song over and went through it without incident.

I smiled throughout the entire process and didn't let it bother me. But I still had to ask myself, "Jerry Lee, what's your point? Do you even have one?"

Just when I thought that he had lost all of the love and tenderness he used to have, he did something I'll never forget. He started playing a song one night in the wrong key, and it was so high that none of us could do the harmonies with him. He stopped playing and asked what the problem was. I thought immediately, "Here we go again."

I replied, "Jerry Lee, you're in the wrong key."

Smug as ever, he asked, "And I suppose you think you could do it better?"

I was not going to give him the satisfaction of thinking he had bested me. I had never played the piano, always concentrating on my singing, but he had recently shown me a boogie run on the piano. Brazenly, I walked over to the piano and started playing this one run that I knew. A run is just a small key segment of a song, and he knew that I couldn't do any more than that one small part. All I could do was just keep repeating it.

He was laughing his ass off at me. Nobody in the audience realized what was going on. He could have just hung me out to dry. Instead, he came over to the bench, sat down beside me, and we played a duet on the piano. I kept repeating the run I knew and he cut loose, making me look far better than I was. When it was over, the audience went wild. I felt him wanting that for me. It was very special, and I remember it to this day.

A wonderful doctor had been treating me for my drug problem and had me on several different drugs to help me through my "drying out" period. I had come to one very firm conclusion — the people out there on the other side of the footlights were a lot happier than we were. I needed to try a different life while I was still alive. I was taking antidepressants and several other pills.

One night, I bottomed out on my entire life. I got down on my knees and prayed to God to help me find a better life. I got up and threw the pills out a window. I didn't take them again after that. Whatever I had to deal with, good or bad, from then on, I wanted to do it clean. Needless, to say, my no-more-drugs attitude didn't set well with Jerry Lee or the band, as they were still hard on them.

I had been out of control without Momma, and I needed to find some sort of foundation to replace the strength I got from her. I found it in the form of a man, Brent Dolan. He was a next-door neighbor in Memphis, and he helped me through this very difficult period. He was all man — handsome, large, strong and mild-mannered with a straight-arrow set of values based in a much more normal world than mine. It seemed to be what I needed. He was extremely shy and, at first, quite nervous around me. Finally, and I thought he'd never get up the nerve, he asked me. "Would you like to go out to supper with me sometime?"

I replied, "When?"

From then on we were a pair. We fell in love and married in 1976. We settled down and I started on my new life as a wife, a real wife, not what I had been before. In all of my previous marriages, though I truly loved most of the men, I never put marriage at the top of my list of priorities. Showbusiness and Jerry Lee Lewis were way in front of anything else in my life. With Brent, I felt I had a relationship that offered something more real than the things I had been chasing for so long. We settled in to a comfortable, working man's lifestyle.

I had two more kids with Brent, Annie and Oliver. My first two children, Cecil Jr., whose father was Cecil Harrelson, and Mary Jean, whose father was Juddy Phillips, Jr., were living with Cecil, and we had become estranged. I loved them dearly, but what kind of mother stays on the road with a rock 'n' roll band? They still harbor bad feelings towards me today, and though I know where they're coming from, it still hurts. I truly love them and I loved their fathers.

Though there is a lot of guilt in a situation like this, if I had it to do all over again, I have no doubt that I would do it the same way. People who are entertainers don't have a choice. It's in their blood and their very makeup. We need the adoration of the crowd, to know that we are good at what we do and recognized for it. I've often said that if somebody came up to me, or probably to any entertainer, and said, "Linda Gail, there's a naked picture of you being circulated in the tabloids," my first reply would no doubt be, "How do I look?" The lifestyle and hardships that come with it are something that we bear for those moments on stage when we are fulfilled. I know it sounds self-serving and cliché, but that's how it is.

With Brent, I spent nine years in three different cities — Memphis, Ferriday and Vale, Tennessee, near Paris. I just wanted to be a wife and mother. I never went around the community saying, "Hi, I'm Linda Gail Lewis, Jerry Lee's sister." That led to one particularly interesting night. We were living in Horn Lake, a community near Memphis, and were playing cards with our neighbors. We played Pitch a lot and were very much accepted as one of the regulars in our neighborhood. I had gotten up to get some drinks for everyone when there was a knock at the door of our small frame cottage. I asked our neighbor, Larry, if he would mind getting the door. He got up and walked over nonchalantly, opening the door and remaining very quiet. Seconds later, he was back in the kitchen proclaiming to his wife, me and Brent, "You ain't goin' to believe this, but Jerry Lee Lewis is standing on your front doorstep!

I replied, "Well, Larry, go let my brother in, for goodness sakes." His face got perfectly white, and then he seemed to flush as he went over to the door and did the honors.

Jerry Lee said that he had come to see Annie, our new

baby girl. That visit was all we heard about for several weeks after that. I think a lot of our neighbors thought Larry had a little too much beer that evening.

Brent never wanted any part of show business. He was a very private, proud man. He drove a truck and did carpenter work, along with raising cows and being a very good father. We didn't have a lot but we were quite happy. Occasionally, Jerry Lee would drop by, and invariably he wanted to help us out. The first old house we bought, he insisted on paying to help fix it up. It needed a roof along with numerous other repairs, and he kicked in several thousand dollars to see that it got done. He never did quit being generous to his family and friends.

Another time he visited with us at Christmas, and after supper, he said, "I've got a present here for you, Linda Gail." I walked over and he handed me a key.

"What's this, Jerry Lee?"

"Why, Linda Gail, those are the keys to the new car I bought for you and Brent. It's parked in the driveway right now." He had bought us a new Chevrolet Celebrity, and it was really needed at the time. Almost everyone has some member of the family that is pretty well-off, some maybe even wealthy. Ask yourself how many of them ever gave you anything like a car, or bought your folks a new house. Jerry Lee made a lot of money, but he was never filthy rich. When he gave something to someone, he felt the loss of the money. It did not come from a never-empty wallet.

After two kids and six years of marriage, we wound up in the little community of Vale, Tennessee. Brent started a little store and called it *Brent and Linda's Country Store.* If you ride through Vale today, you'll see that the store is closed, but our sign is still on the front. I started helping him out waiting on customers and really loved talking with everyone. They eventually found out that Jerry Lee was my brother, and the conversation always came around to what it was like to be on the road with him. I fixed the best lunch sandwiches you ever tasted, and our little store became a "hot spot" of activity. I loved being in the public again.

As good a therapy as this was for me, it also stirred up feelings that I thought had been dead and buried. I was beginning to feel the urge to perform again. The need was still inside of me and a burning started, a burning that hasn't stopped to this day.

Jerry Lee would call or come by and he'd always say, "Linda Gail, when are you coming back on the road with me?"

I'd always say "Never!"

He'd just laugh and say, "You will, you surely will."

The seeds were there, and I felt the desire to perform growing daily. I'd mention my feelings to a few friends at the store, and they would always say, "Go for it, Linda Gail. I'd do it if I was you." Needless to say, Brent did not encourage it at all. I had two young children at home who needed a mother. I finally decided that if I went on a few short trips with Jerry Lee, that I could get it out of my system again.

I told Brent that I wanted to do a few shows before I was too old to try it again. He warned me in the strongest possible terms that he did not want ours to be a show business family. After a great deal of soul searching, I packed a bag, kissed the kids goodbye, and went to catch Jerry Lee at the airport as he was leaving to do a show. "Jerry Lee, I'd really like to go along and do a few shows with you. What do you say?"

He said "That's fine, Linda Gail, you're always welcome." He walked over to a guitar player who was boarding the plane and fired him on the spot to make room for me on the plane. I felt a little bad when that occurred. It took me several minutes to get over it. I was *back on the road!*

By this time, Jerry Lee had married Kerrie McCarver. Kerrie and her sister had been trying to break into show business since they were small children. Their parents were right behind them, pushing all the way. I actually remember seeing them when they were very young. They recorded a version of "Whole Lotta Shakin' Goin' On" when she was nine, and people who knew her as she was growing up tell me that she always said one day she would be Mrs. Jerry Lee Lewis. When Jerry Lee was working clubs around Memphis, she was always there, and before long they were an item. Shawn came into the picture and sidetracked Jerry Lee for a while. Later, after Shawn died, her prophecy was fulfilled when she and Jerry Lee were married. And thus began Jerry Lee's personal version of hell.

I also remember meeting Kerrie's mother, Sarah, for the first time. She told me that she knew that Jerry Lee was a big star and everything, but that she had decided that she would treat him just like everyone else. I immediately thought to myself, treat Jerry Lee Lewis like everybody else is mistake number one.

Kerrie had been doing a few numbers during Jerry Lee's show and had designs on becoming a much larger part of the act. You can just imagine how pleased she was to have me back in the picture. I was making enemies at a record pace. I had barely been on the road for two months when Brent had divorce papers served on me. I actually begged him not to do it. He gave me the proverbial reply, only in reverse: "The highway, or my way!" The truth be told, we were both stepping out on each other at the time. But I still loved him and truly wanted our marriage to work.

You really can't have it all. He wound up marrying my best friend from Vale. She had sat in the store with me so many times encouraging me to go back on the road. I now have to ask myself how far back she had plans for Brent when I went back with Jerry Lee. I was a divorced woman, again. And that was only the beginning of my problems.

Chapter Thirteen: Kerrie KOs Killer's Kid Sister's Kareer

My reunion with Jerry Lee was short-lived, mainly due to Kerrie's objections. She made life miserable for me. She told lies to Jerry Lee about me abusing his money and being extravagant, when just the opposite was true. We finally came to the end of the road and I was fired. And instantly replaced by Kerrie as Jerry Lee's opening act.

I was truly in a mess now. I had no husband, no job, and no marketable skills other than music. And, even if I did, all I wanted to do was sing. I decided that if my brother could go through all the shit he endured to make it, I could face this. I started booking myself in small clubs around Memphis.

One of the first places to risk hiring me was The Bootlegger. I was thrilled to get a gig on my own, even though this was not a high-rent joint. As a matter of fact, it was in a very rough part of town. It was one of those clubs that gave everybody a weapons check at the door. If you didn't have one, they loaned you one. I didn't care. I was in heaven.

Now, I did not play an instrument at the time. I must have been the only Lewis family member who didn't. I determined that I must have some innate genes in me, as closely related as I was to so many great piano players, so I went on a crash course and literally taught myself in short order. At first I just did the basic chords to accompany my singing, but now I have progressed and feel very confident in my talent on the keyboard.

I developed a following around Memphis and began playing some of the better clubs, places like Hernando's Hideaway for owner Kenny Rogers, no relation to the singer. I was also working for Ed Franklin, a veterinarian who owned a bunch of clubs, including Proud Mary's, Bad Bob's and the Vapors. Jerry Lee also played in these clubs when he was in town.

One night he showed up at Hernando's Hideaway to hear me, without telling me. He hadn't seen me on my own yet, and I'm sure he was a little curious. Kenny told me he was there, so I went over to see him. I asked him to come up onstage with me to do a few numbers, but he refused. "I came to see my sister sing, not to sing myself."

I admit that I was extremely nervous playing in front of him. I gave it all I had, and when I returned, he raved about my performance. I'm sure he was being supportive, but I could also tell when he was pumping somebody up, and I realized I had passed his test. He would come and listen to me on numerous occasions after that.

On one particular night, at a club called Mr. Pauls, there was a midget playing the piano and singing. He was terrible, to put it mildly — kind of a Tinier Tim with a piano. Jerry Lee called him over to our table. The little guy was thrilled to think that Jerry Lee had been listening to him play.

Jerry Lee said, "How much are they paying you to play here?"

He replied, "Fifty dollars."

Jerry Lee reached in his pocket, pulled out a stack of bills and said, "Tell you what. I'll give you a hundred to quit playing till I leave." He was crushed but took the money and slipped quietly away.

I told Jerry Lee that it was a pretty cruel thing to do. He shot back, "You don't do anybody a favor by pretending that they've got talent when they don't. They need to be doing something they can be good at in order to be successful." It crossed my mind at that moment to ask how come that rule didn't apply to Kerrie, but I kept my mouth shut.

I don't know why I ever tried to be nice to her. Ed Franklin fired me from the Vapors club, and when I asked him why, he said it was because Kerrie Lewis told him that if I worked for him, Jerry Lee would not be back there. Jerry Lee's appearances there, and they were frequent when he was in town, played a huge part in the club's success, and Ed had no choice but to give in. At that moment, I could have strangled her if I could have gotten my hands around her neck. As a matter of fact, she has *no* body parts small enough for me to get my hands around, and I have pretty damned big hands.

I guess I should have known, having been raised in such a religious family, that if I kept on making bad remarks about the "Kerrie Curse" that Jerry Lee had been stricken with, that I would wind up with one of my own. Poetic justice, I think they call it. It was undoubtedly for that reason that the illustrious Bobby Memphis entered my life.

Bobby was working some of the same clubs that I was. He was, and I'm almost ashamed to admit this, an Elvis impersonator. I know, I know, when I look back on it now, the hairs on the back of my neck stand straight up. First, the term "Elvis impersonator" is an oxymoron, like "military intelligence" — it's a contradiction in terms. No one could ever do credit to Elvis Presley. Jerry Lee was not one to be easily impressed by another performer, but after he saw Elvis' opening night performance at Vegas, he told me, "Linda Gail, Elvis is truly one of the greatest entertainers I've ever seen." It's like someone thinking they can finger-paint the Mona Lisa; it just ain't possible.

But I was alone, scared and needed support. Bobby needed my name. I can look back and see it clearly now. Can you imagine how hard it is to stay booked as an Elvis impersonator? How many times do people want to see someone embarrass themselves? Why he and Kerrie couldn't have met and fallen in love, I'll never know. God does work in mysterious ways. Anyway, I married this guy.

He worked hard at booking me in clubs and when he didn't have a show, he worked on my PA system and the mechanical part of my show. He was good at that sort of thing, and that's a fact. He should have concentrated on being a road manager for a rock group; he would have been a big success. We never loved each other, but we used each other. He used my name much better than I could have done it myself and got us gigs that kept us alive. We played some awfully rough places together. I remember one night when Bobby got in a fight at a club with this huge guy. He had Bobby on a table and was beating him half to death. I guess from seeing my mother take on J.W. Brown that night, the only thing I could do to help him was to take off my high-heel shoe and use it as a weapon. Now, I'm not much of a fighter, but the shoe thing worked out real good. About five good licks on the side of this guy's head and he had enough. A pretty battered Bobby Memphis got up and told me, "Remind me not to piss you off."

I knew that Jerry Lee was huge in Europe and that there was a big revival of the old rockers going on over there. So I decided to try my luck on a European tour. I was actually looking forward to getting away from Bobby. My gigs were getting better and steadier. There were a few people trying to help me, and I was feeling more and more confident that I might actually survive as an artist. Using a few contacts I had made over the years, I literally booked myself on a tour of Europe.

One of the greatest nights of my life as an entertainer occurred in the small country of Wales. I was playing the Jerry Lee Lewis convention in Newport. Now, I made no pretense to myself about why I was able to get booked so easily overseas. Jerry Lee was an absolute god in Europe. He had fan clubs everywhere, and when he made a tour over there every several years, it was always an absolute sellout at every stop. My name was my ticket and I used it.

I knew when I went to sing for this group of several hundred Jerry Lee fans that I was a kind of gimmick act to them, you know, Jerry Lee Lewis' sister. I would always stuff it in till I got on stage, and then I'd forget about everything but the music and I'd let it all hang out. Now, I'm probably not very good at a lot of things that make this world go 'round, but I want to assure you all of one thing — I can rock 'n' roll with the best of them. When I'm done with a song, I leave nothing behind. I give it all I've got and the audience can tell it.

This night, in this tiny little country, thousands of miles away from home, I got onstage as a sideshow, but when I finished, they knew I was for real. I got a standing ovation that lasted five minutes.

Completely drained, I went to the lounge to get a cold drink and meet some of the fans. They were wonderful to me and so appreciative. As we started to get to know one another, someone who had taped my entire show put the video in the television over the bar, and believe it or not, we all watched the entire show over again. And they gave me a five-minute standing ovation again. It was one of the greatest feelings of my life. I knew then that I was on the right course again.

I made many friends all over Europe but especially in Norway, which has become almost a second home for me. One of my best friends, Stephen Ackles, is a big star there. We have been extremely close ever since my first tour there. He books me and I stay at his home with his family when I'm there. I've even been taking my now-grown daughter Annie with me, and she has also fallen in love with the country and the people.

Chapter Fourteen:

Click the Blue Suede Heels Together Three Times, Bobby

During this period, I had been working with Eddie Braddock, a well-known promoter from Memphis. Eddie had been the driving force behind the blues label Stax Records in Memphis, and he had a string of acts a mile long to his credit. He began managing my career and offered a stability and credibility that helped me turn the corner as a solo act. He reminded me a lot of Cecil Harrelson — a real man, steady, quiet and handsome. He was a no-bullshit kind of person, and a Born Again Christian. His beliefs were a lot like my mother's. His attitude was, "I'm married and I don't run around." I think I fell in love with him from day one.

We worked together on and off for three years. He was very successful and lived with his wife on a beautiful estate with fishing ponds and a magnificent home. He had everything all wrapped up in a beautiful little package. We started spending a great deal of time together, and he even accompanied me on a European tour, much to the displeasure of his wife, whom he had assured that he was through with the record business. He was retired and working with Federal Express. She put the squeeze on him and said, "It's either Linda Gail or me." He apparently valued our relationship more than all his possessions and opted for getting out of the marriage. I truly loved him and wanted to marry him also.

I was staying with Stephen Ackles in Norway when the decision was made. I looked at him and said, "As cold as it is here today, I think this is a good time to call Bobby." I was still married to Bobby Memphis, though he remained in Tennessee. I got him on the phone, and the first words out of his mouth were, "When are you coming home?"

My answer was, "I'm not, Bobby. I want a divorce."

He then shot back, "It's that son of a bitch Eddie Braddock, isn't it?"

I guess it was apparent to everyone that we were looking hard at each other.

I got back into Memphis on a weekend, and on Monday morning I called my old friend Jim Sanderson, a well-respected attorney. This was in December 1991. I said to him over the phone, "Jim, I want you to get me a divorce this week so I can get married next weekend." It was Monday and I wanted to get married on Saturday. Jim's reply was quite predictable. "God damn, Linda Gail! It's Monday and you want a divorce by Friday? Who do you think I am?" I knew he was well connected and I reminded him of that fact. I ended it with, "I want a damn divorce and I want it now!"

He asked me, "Well, Linda Gail, just who is it you're wanting to marry now?" I told him it was Eddie Braddock. He suggested a bargain that he would make.

"Linda Gail, I loved your Momma. She was a fine woman, and I'll do this for her and you if you'll make me a promise. I know Eddie Braddock and he's a good man. If you'll promise me that you will stay with him, I'll do it, this one time." I told him I loved Eddie and he would be the last man I would marry. The deal was struck.

Jim Sanderson had a friend who was a judge, and he decided that he would need a favor to pull this off. He also told me that it could be done only if Bobby Memphis didn't contest it. It would have to be by mutual consent. I called Bobby and told him that if he would grant me a divorce, I would let him keep all the stuff we had accumulated during our marriage. We weren't rich, but we had a nice van, a lot of band equipment and some money saved up. And Bobby was a pretty greedy guy.

I also told him, "You're an adulterer. You know it and I know it. You've run around on me the whole time we've been married, and I can prove it. If you contest me on this divorce, it will take a long time to go through court, and I promise you that you'll leave with nothing but your drawers. If you want all this shit, you can have it, but you'll have to come with me to court and tell the judge that you don't object to the divorce." He knew I meant it.

We went from Bolivar to Selma, a town in McNairy County. This is the place where the sheriff who was immortalized in the movie *Walking Tall* actually lived, and the events occurred there. Incidentally, in this town, Jim not only was great friends with the judge, but the judge was a Jerry Lee fan who had actually played a mailman in the movie *Great Balls of Fire*. This judge was willing to go along with the program, but he said he wanted another judge to represent Bobby so that he could never come back on him. We were to take Bobby over to this other judge, and Bobby would have to swear to him that he wanted the divorce too.

I picked up Bobby and we drove first over to Jim Sanderson's house. He lived in this gorgeous mansion and had a very high-end party in progress when we arrived. We were escorted in and Bobby started falling apart. Jim introduced me to all of these rich folks who were dressed like a high school formal and drinking champagne as they walked over to shake my hand.

Now, beside me, this weird looking Elvis impersonator with dyed black hair and mutton-chop sideburns was bawling his eyes out, saying, "Linda Gail, I know I was unfaithful but I do love you. Please don't leave. I'll die. Please, God, oh, please don't leave me." As he continued, the tears ran down his face, and he sobbed out loud.

The folks at the party acted as if he were non-existent, making lighthearted conversation with me, very cordially, with their cocktails still in their hands. "So nice to meet you, Linda Gail. Won't you stay and meet everyone?" It was straight out of "Saturday Night Live." Jim noticed the act that Bobby had going and pulled me aside.

"Linda Gail, if he acts like this over at this judge's place, you're fucked! You better set him straight real quick, or this is going to fall apart in our faces." I assured him I would and that Bobby would be fine at the judge's. I got Bobby back in the car, still crying and moaning how this was killing him, and a quick plan came to mind.

As luck would have it, one of the state's actual nut houses was in Bolivar. It was a building straight out of a Stephen King novel — a large, old Victorian gothic building that made the Bates Motel look like a Holiday Inn. I was always astounded that they would take people who were already crazy and put them in a place that would scare the shit out of them! I drove Bobby by this house of horrors and said, "Bobby, do you see this place?"

"Yes, I see it. Boo-hoo," crying ever harder. "I see it. What about it?"

"Bobby, I'm taking you over to meet this judge, and if you act crazy like you're doing right now, we're going to put you in that place for about a year. Do you understand me?" He looked real hard at the place and straightened right up.

"I do," was all he said. We went to the judge's house, and he asked Bobby if he wanted this divorce, and he replied, "I do. I think it's for the best." He was as straight as a Holiness preacher.

Friday came and the divorce was on the court docket. I was scared to death that something was going to go wrong and screw it all up. The courtroom was jam-packed with people on all sorts of matters, most of which were undoubtedly more important than my divorce. Hell, there were people in there who would be going to jail that night. You could see the concern on everyone's face. I was dreading the whole thing.

I had never spent any time in a courtroom. In all of my previous divorces, the only one I tried to get a divorce from was Kenny Lovelace, and it turned out that we weren't even legally married, so I didn't need to get it. The rest of the time, I just left and never worried about a divorce. They always got one so they could move on with their lives.

So, you see the picture here. This real stern looking judge was handed my papers by Jim Sanderson as the first order of business. My name was called and I went to the front of the courtroom, sweating more than I ever did on national television or at a concert in front of 10,000 fans. I was waiting for the judge to start grilling me in front of all these people when he looked at me and said, "Divorce granted."

I replied, "Thank you, your honor."

I turned to leave the courtroom and he yells back to me, "You know, I was in the movie *Great Balls of Fire.*

"I do. That's wonderful, sir."

He continued, "I can play 'Great Balls of Fire' on the piano. Did Jim tell you that?"

"No, sir, he didn't."

"It's a fact. I'm a hell of a piano player."

Everyone in the courtroom was staring in unbelievably stunned silence as this bizarre conversation continued. This had to be the strangest divorce in the history of organized court proceedings.

Next we had to visit the Clerk of Court's office to get a new marriage license. When would this all end? This office was in Germantown. The woman who ran the place was in a sixties time warp with her bouffant hairdo and horned-rim glasses. She was very proper acting as she demanded, "Next!" We approached her and she started asking questions as she filled out the papers.

First she turned to Eddie. "Now, how many marriages will this be for you?"

Eddie replied, "Four." She looked down at him through her glasses as if to infer, "Creep."

"And how long have you been divorced?"

"About four weeks."

"I don't think that's long enough, sir."

"Well, I have a paper here from the judge that says it is." She got snootier by the second.

"Oh, I see. There is a time limit, you know. I suppose the judge can waive it if he wants, even though it's not really very ethical."

She turned to me. She got my name and birthday and all the basics. I knew it was coming.

"And how many marriages will this be for you, miss?"

"This is, er . . . uh, number eight."

"EIGHT!"

Eddie snapped back at her. "She said eight." There was unpleasantness in his voice.

Now defensive, she inquired, "And when was your last divorce granted?"

"December 7th, 1991."

She did a double take and then gasped, "That's today! You can't get married this quick."

"The judge said we could."

"Well, you're going to have to get the judge to sign this document for you, because I'm not going to do it. It's not legal or ethical." She handed me the document.

I was in no mood to go back up to Boliver and ask that judge to put me back on the court agenda just to get this piece of paper signed. Eddie went to a local restaurant and got a sandwich. I got a pen, signed the damn thing myself and took it back to the old biddy.

"Here, it's signed."

She studied for a full minute, then she signed it too and gave us our marriage license. We were married on Pearl Harbor Day, December 7th, 1991, the same afternoon my divorce was granted. True to my word to Jim Sanderson, we are still married today and just as much in love as on our wedding day.

Chapter Fifteen:
Let Me Interrupt Myself

When I woke up this morning and started thinking back over the stories in this book, I was overcome with a feeling of sadness. Jerry Lee Lewis, the greatest living entertainer, sits walled up in the bedroom of his home in Memphis.

By my own appraisal, he is still heavily under the influence of drugs, more than likely Demerol on prescription from a groupie doctor. I was told that it was Methadone and that he had kicked all the hard stuff. It might be so, but he's just not right. His daughter Phoebe visited me recently and expressed her concern for him. It was her feeling that his single biggest problem is depression.

Jerry Lee's present wife Kerrie, and her father Bob McCarver, or "The General" as he likes to be called (in a gesture of superiority to a lower ranking Colonel Tom Parker who managed Elvis), control every breath that Jerry Lee takes.

I suspect Jerry Lee doesn't have a clue about how much money he made last year. Kerrie and her father are, in my opinion, milking him for all they can. If that's not enough to cause him to be severely depressed, I don't know what is.

Jerry Lee has to have a metal door to his bedroom, like a prison, because Kerrie runs tours through the house they live in. For only $12 you can tour Jerry Lee's home and see how truly fucked up his life is. On one occasion Kerrie was not there to greet the tour bus, and so Jerry Lee showed up — in his underpants, beer in hand — and personally conducted the tour. When he had finished escorting everyone through his home, he took them to the back room where Kerrie keeps items such as records, videos and souvenirs that she hawks to the tourists. When they wanted to buy some, Jerry Lee didn't know how much to charge, so he just invited them "take what you want." When Kerrie got back and saw that the place had been cleaned out for no money, she went ballistic.

I was visiting with him one day as one of these "tours" went through and a forlorn looking Jerry Lee said to me, "Linda Gail, would you look at this? Kerrie is turning my house into some sort of tourist trap, another Graceland. Only I ain't even dead yet!" It was so sad it was funny.

The only reason that Jerry Lee puts up with all this shit is his beautiful son, Lee. He is ten now and a little angel. After losing Jerry Lee, Jr., two of his wives and, of course, our parents, Jerry Lee is extremely protective of Lee. He truly believes that the way he has lived has caused God to take loved ones from him, and that if he steps too much out of line now, Lee will be the next. This is not an exaggeration. Jerry Lee still has his Holiness Church upbringing tearing at his conscience and soul every waking minute. At least Lee gives him some enjoyment. Jerry Lee actually gets up and takes him to Little League practice and games and demands that Lee be taken to church every Sunday. This fact, even more than Jerry Lee's advancing age, has made his home a lot more pleasant place. All of the riotous events of the past are not occurring there at this point in his life.

It is no secret to anyone who knows Jerry Lee's present situation that I am not welcome there. Not by Jerry Lee — I know that he loves me — but because Kerrie flat out doesn't want me, or anyone who might exert some measure of influence over Jerry Lee, having any access to him. He is completely under her control, and she has made it very clear that if he doesn't walk the line, she will leave and Lee will go with her. Jerry Lee does not want to lose this last child, and he will do whatever it takes to keep him.

Recently Jerry Lee was in Nashville, where I live at the present, and Kerrie and everyone associated with Jerry Lee went to great pains to keep it a secret from me. That hurts me deeply. I was raised with Jerry, and I traveled with him for more than fifteen years, opening his shows. I would be willing to wager that no one has ever had as close a relationship with Jerry Lee as I have, and I'm sure that closeness is the very reason Kerrie doesn't want me having any contact with him. She's got the goose that laid the golden eggs by the balls, and she intends to keep him there.

Jerry Lee has never been the Elvis type of recluse. He gets in his car and goes anywhere in Memphis he wants to. You could easily be in a store shopping and have him get in line behind you. And he has always appreciated his fans. If you spoke to him, you would get the sort of polite, interested answer that you might expect from a country boy from Ferriday. He is still besieged by requests for interviews but he is generally on guard against discussing his private life with anyone.

There was a reporter from the *National Inquirer* who had bugged the hell out of him to do a book on his life. Reluctantly, Jerry Lee agreed to see him. He came to Memphis and sat in the living room of the house for five full days. Jerry Lee never spoke to him once during that time, even though he was living in the house the entire time. Finally, discouraged by Jerry's total lack of cooperation, the reporter packed up and went back to Florida.

Not too long ago, when I had gotten on Jerry severely about why he would continually fuck his life up with drugs and all the self-destructive things he does, he told me it was because he was "bored." He said "I've done everything, there's nothing I haven't done, and I'm just bored, Linda Gail." I think that may add a little backbone to the theory that he is depressed.

This is not to say that Jerry Lee's existence is completely miserable. He still lives an extremely luxurious lifestyle. The home he and Kerrie have is gorgeous. There are a lot of toys, and Lee gives him great satisfaction. Kerrie did get Jerry Lee's much publicized problems with the Internal Revenue Service squared away, and he at least has a home life — as weird as it might seem to anyone else. But Jerry Lee isn't like anyone else. With all that has happened to him in his life, he couldn't be.

I understand that he grossed over a million dollars in 1995 before he and his booking agent parted ways. He's not working much now, but I'm sure he could be booked just as much as he wants. There's always Las Vegas. Jerry and Las Vegas have a love-hate relationship: Every time he plays there, he does something outrageous, and they swear they'll never have him back again. The next year, he's back. Maybe at another club, but there is still a strong public demand to see him, and it's worldwide.

The last time he played Las Vegas was particularly bizarre. Jerry had a long-time running gag with a piano stool — he would always destroy the stool before the show was over. On his last show there, they decided to fix him and had a piano bench specially made out of steel. It was virtually indestructible.

Jerry was already high as a kite before he came on stage. He got into a war with the bench and eventually wound up on the floor of the stage wrestling with the thing . . . much to the delight of a crowd that expected such strange behavior from Jerry Lee. One of the band members said he timed him and that he wrestled with the stool for a full twenty minutes. That finished, Jerry Lee returned to the piano.

While he had been wrestling with the stool, he had noticed a large table of Japanese tourists sitting at a prominent front-row table. Unbelievably, he stopped playing and said out loud, "Who let in these squelchy-eyed motherfuckers down front here?" He continued, "Hell, I ain't forgot Pearl Harbor. I ain't playing another damn note till you get the hell out of here."

Needless to say, everyone was stunned. The casinos understand only too well the tons of money dropped there ever year from visiting Orientals, and they were none too forgiving of the remarks. Jerry Lee's next show that night, as well as the rest of the gig, was canceled along with accompanying promises of "You'll never play Vegas again." Jerry Lee has had that said to him every time he's ever played there, but I'm sure he'll be back there again soon.

I think so many of Jerry's problems come from all the tragedy he has seen. There is no doubt that he never got over the loss of Momma. Sometimes I think that it hurts him to see me because I remind him so much of her. Jerry has been everywhere, seen and done just about everything. He's done a lot of good for a lot of people . . . and a lot of crazy shit he shouldn't have done.

Coupled with his present home-life and not the best of health, I have a lot of reason to be concerned for my brother. After all, he took me out of a horribly poor childhood in the middle of nowhere and showed me the world. I'm far better off for having had him as a brother, and I will always wish only the best for him.

Chapter Sixteen:
Where Are We?

Today I commute between our rural home in Big Sandy, Tennessee, and Nashville. I periodically do tours of Europe, where I've always received a bigger response than in the United States. I am as happy as I have ever been. My two children by Brent, Annie and Oliver live with Eddie and me. Eddie never had children of his own, but he has accepted my children by other men as his and unselfishly gives his time and love to them. I think it is the mark of a great man to be able to raise and care for children by previous husbands. Eddie has been supportive of me, my career and my dreams. I hope we are buried side by side under the big trees on our farm.

My sister Frankie Jean is still in Ferriday. She runs the Lewis Family Museum there and several other businesses. She's smart and good with money, like Jimmy Swaggart and Mickey Gilley. She even operates a drive-through store that is famous for selling anything from a box of popcorn to large mixed drinks right to your car. Jerry Lee is still close with Frankie and has not allowed Kerrie to sue her for using his likeness and name on everything from photos to drinking glasses which she sells to tourists at her museum and store. She has a happy, stable family, and I'm very proud of her.

And Jerry Lee? I haven't seen him or talked to him in almost a year. I would like for us to be close again. I miss him.

If you have never seen Jerry Lee in concert, and you love music, you owe it to yourself to go hear him while you still can. He is the master of his craft and one of the last surviving founders of rock 'n' roll. No matter about any shortcomings in his personal life or failures in things other than music, he brings to a song raw emotions based in experience. He combines his country roots, his soul and rhythm and blues influences, and the personal heartbreaks he has known into a unique delivery that says, "I've been there." He has. I know it because I was there with him. The Devil, me, and Jerry Lee.